Professor Birdsong's

Weird Criminal Law Stories

Volume II

Stories from Around the States and Abroad

Leonard Birdsong

Winghurst Publications

Professor Birdsong's Weird Criminal Law Stories - Volume II - Stories from Around the States and Abroadby Leonard Birdsong

© 2013Leonard Birdsong

ISBN: 978-0-9972964-4-0 (CreateSpace 2016)
ISBN: 978-0-9979573-0-3 (Kindle)

Winghurst Publications
1969 S. Alafaya Trail / Suite 303
Orlando, FL 32828-8732
www.BirdsongsLaw.com
lbirdsong@barry.edu

Disclaimer:
The facts that are recounted in the stories in this volume are true and in the public domain, as best as Professor Birdsong can determine from his research of court documents, newspapers, and wire services. The author's commentaries on these stories are his own views and opinions and do not reflect the official policy or position of any Law school, Law firm or other organization with which the author may be affiliated. The opinions provided herein are not intended to malign or defame any religion, ethnic group, club, organization, company, individual or anyone or anything. The author further covenants and represents that the work contains no matter that will incite prejudice, amount to an invasion of privacy, be libelous, obscene or otherwise unlawful or which infringe upon any proprietary interest at common law, trademark, trade secret, patent or copyright. The author is the sole proprietor of the work and all parts thereof.

Permissions:
Cover graphic: ©CoryThoman|Dreamstime.com, ©Madartists|Dreamstime.com
Book cover design: Rik Feeney / Rik@PublishingSuccessOnline.com

Table of Contents

INTRODUCTION

Professor Leonard Birdsong lives in Orlando, Florida where he teaches Criminal Law, White Collar Crime, Evidence and Immigration Law. He has written many scholarly legal articles since joining the legal academy. His latest scholarly piece is entitled: *Reforming the Immigration Courts of the United States: Why Is There No Will to Make It An Article I Court?*

This publication is not one of those scholarly pieces!

This second volume of Weird Criminal Law Stories is written just for fun and for your enjoyment.

Although he has been involved in serious criminal law work over the years as a prosecutor, a defense attorney, and a law professor, Professor Birdsong knows that it is good to get a good laugh at least once every day. That is why several years ago he began to collect and edit from the wire services and other news outlets the type of weird criminal law stories that appear in this volume.

Professor Birdsong wishes to thank his sharp-eyed and brilliant student research assistants, Erin Sperger and Carissa Aponte, for their excellent editorial assistance on this volume.

Professor Birdsong hopes that you will get a few good laughs from this his second collection, of his Weird Criminal Law Stories and his commentary accompanying each of them.

Enjoy!

CHAPTER ONE

WEIRD CRIMINAL LAW STORIES FROM CALIFORNIA AND OUT WEST

CALIFORNIA: A paraplegic man is suing two stores in a California shopping mall after they refused to let him inside accompanied by his service animal. The animal happened to be a minihorse. The 29 inch pony pulled the man's wheelchair and he is seeking $4,000 from each of the businesses.

....Service minihorse? Did the stores fear horse droppings?

CALIFORNIA: Here's a law suit for you. Republicans are suing a California congressional candidate, claiming that astronaut Jose Hernandez should not be allowed to list "astronaut" under his name on the ballot. There is no dispute that Democrat Hernandez flew on the shuttle Discovery in

2009. However, the law suit claims that "astronaut is not a title one carries for life."

Bet you John Glenn disputes that contention...

IDAHO: Upon being arrested in Twin Falls, Dylan Contreras maintained he was not the man named in the arrest warrant. However, police noticed his forearm tattoo that clearly spelled out the name "Dylan Contreras."

If the tattoo fits then you cannot acquit!

CALIFORNIA: There may be some truth to the rumor that Ninja marijuana bandits are on the loose in the suburbs of LA. A man delivering medical marijuana maintains he was robbed recently by two men dressed as ninjas in West Covinia. The delivery man said the ninjas took his pot and his cash.

Ninjas my foot...Bet this was an inside job!

ARIZONA: A convicted killer begged for mercy at his sentencing in Phoenix. He told the judge, "I regret every moment of the day I beat a 90 year old man to death." His family was by his side and he said that he planned to change his life and leave prison as a better man. He then undermined his own case by turning around and flipping the finger to a television camera person. He received a 22 year sentence.

Dunce!

NEW MEXICO: The town of Vaughn has a small police department of just two; neither of the two officers is allowed to carry a gun because of legal problems. The chief lost his gun over a child support issue and his deputy can't carry because of a domestic violence incident. The chief said not having a gun was no problem, "We have Tasers, batons, mace…stuff like that."

N-Sane... Police sans guns!

TEXAS: Houston resident Natalie Plummer was arrested for holding up a sign alerting drivers to a speed trap. She did 12 hours in jail. Why? Police held her on an obscure charge of standing in the street where there's a sidewalk present – a misdemeanor.

...The police have to make their quota of tickets!

IDAHO: A courthouse was evacuated when a suspicious package showed up and starting beeping. After sending in the bomb squad, officials discovered the package contained a magazine with a greeting card style musical insert.

No Ka-Boomee....

OREGON: We learn that two employees of a Portland firm were awarded $332,000 after a jury found that they had been wrongly fired after they complained to authorities about having to use a bucket to urinate, since no bathroom was available on the premises. The report concluded that the two are "now flush with buckets of money."

What a whizz...

MONTANA: A Billings police officer is in trouble for driving two drunken citizens outside the city limits and leaving them in the cold January air by the side of the road to sober up at 3 am. It did not work! The man and woman "were very intoxicated and stumbled into traffic," authorities report. We now learn that Officer Paul Lamantia is looking forward to his two week suspension.

Paul, you are a chucklehead!

CALIFORNIA: Police call it grand theft Fido. Police are looking for the thief who stole a $27,000 show dog. The 18 month old, 175 pound Great Dane was stolen from an RV that was parked during a trip to a dog show.

Police may find the pooch on Craigslist...It's kind of difficult to overlook a Great Dane.

UTAH: A teen from Orem will have an easy time convincing his teacher that he has an excuse for not turning in his homework. Police will back up his story, too. Why? The 18 year old accidently left a computer hard drive containing his assignment in the back yard of a home he allegedly had just burglarized.

D'OH!!!!

TEXAS: A man from the town of Kemah was arrested for riding his unicycle completely naked. He told police he liked the feeling of riding without any clothes on. Police said he was distracting other drivers.

The police could see he's nuts…

TEXAS: A Lewisville man reportedly went postal when one of his two dogs defecated in the house. Michael Stephens, 76, shot and killed his wife and both of his dogs upon finding the dog mess. He then held off police in a five hour standoff before he was arrested.

WOOF….

OREGON: A Medford man wanted some peace and quiet in his trailer park and thought the best way to get it was by firing a handgun at two youngsters, 9 and 14 years old at play. It is reported that Danny Way, 42, stood about ten feet away, aimed his 9mm into the air over their heads and squeezed off several shots. As you might guess, police charged him with menacing, reckless endangerment, disorderly conduct and unlawful use of a weapon.

What an idiot!

ARIZONA: A principal of a charter school was forced to resign and his secretary was fired after a 16 year old student used her smart phone to make a video of the two making out. We learn further that the video by 16 year old Myranda Garber at the school in the town of Quartzsite caused a scandal because both the principal and the secretary have spouses.

There must be no canoodling in school…

TEXAS: Jesus Ventura, 37, appears to have been raised to have good manners. He allegedly robbed a Chase bank branch in Dallas and then slipped the teller $20 and said, "Here's a tip for you." Ventura, ran off but was stopped by an off duty fireman He was subsequently arrested and faces federal bank robbery charges.

…Always say please and thank you and leave a tip!

TEXAS: A judge ordered a drunken driver, who served 90 days in jail, for killing a man in a crash to spend four consecutive Saturdays at the crash scene in suburban

Houston wearing a sign that read: "I killed Aaron Coy Pennywell while driving drunk." Michael Giancona, 38, must also hang a picture taken at the scene of the 2011 crash in his living room.

Not a stiff sentence but maybe he will be shamed into sobriety.

CALIFORNIA: A scientist at the University of California San Diego, who received a $200 traffic ticket, prepared a long treatise that used physics and math to demonstrate how he might have actually come to a full halt at a stop sign he had been accused of running. The judge found in his favor, but said it was not the science that got him off. Judge Karen Riley admitted the paper was too complicated for her to understand. However, she decided the officer who gave him the ticket had been too far away to have gotten a good view of what happened.

Mr. Brainiac wins…

TEXAS: Recently a convicted sex offender, Adam Mabery, just released from prison allegedly broke into a Goodwill Thrift Store in the town of Sherman and modeled a red dress, purse and heels. Surveillance cameras recorded the intoxicated Mabery dancing and bleeding from the broken glass around the store.

Yes Adam, life can be a "drag" if you let it...

CALIFORNIA: They call him a dumbbell! A weight lifter in Modesto suffered a gunshot wound while exercising. He said he accidently dropped his dumbbell on a bullet, causing it to fire into his shoulder. Police say the story is suspicious, but not impossible.

What kind of gym has bullets lying around?

COLORADO: When a woman at the Denver International Airport was told to extinguish her cigarette she freaked out and took off all her clothes, according to a police report. The woman told police she was on edge and had not slept the night before. She was taken to a local hospital. No charges were lodged.

On edge is one thing, getting naked is another!

CALIFORNIA: Moments after San Francisco Judge Lillian Sing let car burglar Phillip Bernard off with just a warning, the bad boy smashed open the rear window of a vehicle parked outside the courthouse. It just so happens that the car was owned by Judge Sing. Bernard, 32, was arrested and is now behind bars.

Proves no good deed goes unpunished... Ironic, no?

CALIFORNIA: Cornell Jackson and Marquet Dorsey, both more than 200 pounds and six feet tall, went through the trouble of wearing dresses and makeup to scam stores in a scheme involving prepaid credit cards. When one of the "perp's" cards would be declined, the other man would quickly call the store pretending to represent the credit card company and authorize the purchase. Police report the scheme did not work out well and both were arrested.

Two silly cretins in drag...

TEXAS: Carrie King, 34, called Galveston police to report an intruder in her home.

When police arrived they walked in on King furiously blasting away at Elvis Alexander, 53, with her paintball gun. Alexander was covered in yellow paint, but was otherwise uninjured as police took him into custody.

KA-Pow, Ka-Pow, Ka-Pow....

TEXAS: Cynthia Creed, 51, had just been dismissed from jury duty in Houston when she texted a co-worker: "Call the courthouse. Tell them there is a bomb." Then, 15 minutes later she texted, "Just kidding." However, the co-worker had already called the police who evacuated the courthouse. Creed was arrested for giving a false police report.

Cynthia is a nincompoop...

CALIFORNIA: A Modesto man showed up drunk for his court date on a previous public intoxication charge. Ryan Nunes, then created a disturbance and refused to leave the courtroom – he was arrested again.

Where is "AA" when a guy really needs them?

TEXAS: A man found his stolen car after 42 years! Bob Russell, 68, found his beloved Austin-Healey 3000 for sale on eBay. The racing car was stolen in 1970 when Russell was in school in Philadelphia. He got it back after a legal battle with a California dealer that had already received a bid of $19,000 for the car on the online auction site.

Should we call him "Mr. Lucky?"

IDAHO: A lady attempting to evacuate from a wild fire near her Colorado Springs home wound up driving to Idaho – where she started another fire after she crashed her car into a field. The second fire scorched 2,000 acres and made the woman one of the less popular recent Idaho visitors.

She's a real hot mama....

TEXAS: A buck-naked driver caused a commotion when he smashed his pickup truck through the front entrance doors of the Southwest Center Mall in Dallas. He emerged from the damage vehicle, walked over to the Champs Sports outlet and started donning clothes from the rack until police arrived and nabbed him.

What a naked loser...Ewww... Do you think they'll still sell those garments?

NEW MEXICO: A clumsy burglar in Albuquerque was arrested after he tried to break into a college office and became tangled up in the venetian blinds as he crawled through a window. The accused burglar, Thomas Molina, who was allegedly trying to steal computers became so entangled that he had to be helped out of the blinds bind by police before being taken off to jail.

El stupido y crudo, perhaps....

OREGON: A Salem woman was arrested after she allegedly told police she suspected that her 17 year old daughter was stripping at a local club. An investigation found video of the mother at the club watching her daughter's routine and even giving her money. Christina Marie Lopez, 42, has now been charged with sexual exploitation of a minor.

Dirty Dancing...

WASHINGTON STATE: A man was arrested after he tried to steal a vibrating condom, lubricant and mascara from a drug store in Seattle. According to the police report, when a store security guard tried to stop him, the man tried to beat him with brass knuckles before shocking the guard with a Taser.

A vibrating condom, lubricant, and mascara? Why? We guess he wanted to party with himself...

WASHINGTON STATE: Police gave a ticket to a motorist who was using a special car pool lane that required he have at least one passenger. However, his only companion was a skeleton dressed in a white sweat shirt. The motorist told police he decided on the skeleton after he rejected the idea of sharing the front seat with a blowup doll or a mannequin.

He should have told the police she was his anorexic girlfriend...

WASHINGTON STATE: We learn that police took down and arrested a cocaine trafficker that was so proud of his vocation that he sported vanity plates on his car that read, "SMUGGLER." The police also found the trafficker's car loaded with 24 pounds of narcotics parked near the Canadian border at a hotel named The Smuggler's Inn.

Are we starting to see a pattern of why he got caught?

TEXAS: Littlefield, an insolvent Texas town solved its debt problem by selling its jail. A private prison firm paid $6 million for the Bill Clayton Detention Center in Littlefield, beating out two other bidders.

Are there that many people looking to buy jails?

OREGON: Merry Christmas! A man in the town of Aloha, Oregon broke into a couple's home and attacked them with a tiki torch on Christmas morning 2011. The man who was dressed only in his underwear, socks and a bandana and during the attack he swung the Hawaiian style torch at the residents. When the male victim pulled out a gun, the intruder batted it out of his hand with the tiki torch and fled. Police report the torch wielder appeared to have been on drugs.

You think....

OREGON: A Portland man was in so much of a hurry to get to court in time for his trial on meth possession charges that he received three speeding tickets totaling $2,000. The man, Jose Romero-Valenzula, was reportedly pulled over three times for going 105 mph, then 98 mph and 92 mph. He was in a rush to get to trial, in order to show the judge he had kicked his drug habit.

Zoom Zoom

UTAH: Talk about karma. Eldon Alexander, 36 and Korin Vanhouten, 47, of Ogden had just been cited and released on shoplifting charges when they returned to their car – and found someone had broken into it. Their stereo and amplifier, a drum machine and cigarettes worth about $60 had been stolen. The couple had just been cited for pilfering $25 worth of goods.

Yes, Lord, what goes around comes around – again and again…

MONTANA: We learn that John Hughes of Butte always wanted to know how it felt to be the object of a police chase. So, he drove around one day looking for a police car. When he found one he sped off at 100 mph. He was indeed chased and caught. In addition to having to pay a fine, he has to buy new tires. Police stopped him by using a "spike strip."

Bet he is glad he got that out of his system!

COLORADO: It has been reported that a 46 year old man is being suspected of being Denver's mysterious "crapper scrapper." Donal Allen Citron is suspected of perpetrating 18 burglaries in the first three months of 2012 by walking into the restrooms of various businesses, ripping copper or brass plumbing and hardware from the toilets and sticking the metal in his backpack.

"Crapper scrapper" has a ring about it, no…

COLORADO: What a way to go. Warehouse worker Raymond Segura, Jr. died in March at the storage warehouse of the Kelley Bean Co. in the town of Brush when he was buried under 15 feet of pinto beans. The beans were brought into the storage unit on an overhead conveyor belt, but it was unclear how Segura, 56, came to be crushed by them.

Death by pinto beans! Ain't that a gas…

TEXAS: We learn that a ranking official in the town of Keller decided that he wasn't needed. As a result of this revelation he laid himself off. City manager Dan O'Leary, who was paid $176,000 a year, said two others do the same work and a third wasn't needed.

What a Robin Hood!

TEXAS: Thieves snatched a 500 pound beehive packed with 5,000 angry bees from outside a Houston restaurant which used the insects to make honey. It may have been a sting operation.

Bzzz Bzzz…What honeynuts…

HAWAII: A 64 year old Hawaiian lawyer was found guilty of licking a 21-year-old former client on the back of her ear. Lihue federal judge Lawrence McCreery fined the lawyer $250 and told him, “These are the actions of a dirty old man.”

No, lawyers are not allowed to lick their clients!

TEXAS: In 2012 a Houston man finally paid off his parking ticket from February 2, 1953. Abe Crawford, 79, dropped off his 1946 Nash automobile at a metered spot before shipping out to fight in Korea. His father was late in picking up the vehicle, leading to the ticket. Crawford had recently found the old, unpaid ticket in a box of keepsakes and arranged to pay the $1 fine

A *Real life “Honest Abe.”*

ARIZONA: A 20 year old Tempe man was caught at a pet shop stuffing two tarantulas down his pants before walking out. Authorities do not believe the crime was spontaneous because he had been seen in the store checking out the tanks previously by employees.

Boxers or Briefs???

NEW MEXICO: Police in Albuquerque caught a prison parolee trying to flee to Mexico after he decided he did not want to take a drug test. With him was his fiancée. Police did not want to disappoint the love birds, so they arranged for a justice of the peace to come to the gas station where the pair had been stopped for a wedding ceremony where the groom wore handcuffs. Shortly after the ceremony the man was taken to jail.

What, no time for a Honeymoon?

OREGON: A Portland man allegedly hid his girlfriend in a large suitcase with wheels and smuggled her into his apartment building for a visit. The 50-year-old girlfriend had been barred from his building for over a year after she smashed a fire extinguisher during a lover's quarrel. The 96 pound woman was arrested this time for trespass.

The headline read: "This guy had a lot of baggage"

OREGON: A trucker in Oregon who got too drunk to drive called his dispatcher and reported that he was being held at gunpoint. His dispatcher called the police who soon found the truck, as well as the drunken liar nearby.

Just another drunken dummy!

NEW MEXICO: A beagle in the town of Gallup went for a walk and came back with possible evidence in a murder case, a human skull. Police determined the skull was that of a man 35 to 45 years old who had probably been dead two to three years. "It's a criminal investigation…until we determine otherwise," said Deputy Police Chief John Allen.

WOOF WOOF...Sounds like a stone "Who done it."

CALIFORNIA: Police Arrested an Oregon man for allegedly carrying $1 million in crystal meth at a bus terminal in, of all places, Weed, California. Martin Chavez, 49, had 12 duct tape wrapped packages of the drug in a suitcase, police maintain.

The headline read: "Wrong City Wrong Drug." Amen!

CALIFORNIA: A San Diego bank robber broke a rule of robbery – don't flee the robbery with vanity plates on your auto. The alleged robber pulled a gun at a teller window and fled on foot with $3,000. Witnesses advised police they saw him climb into a white Ford Expedition with the personalized license plate that read: ALM DUDE. The vehicle was registered to Robert Alm, 27, who was quickly arrested.

Dude, you're an idiot!

CALIFORNIA: We learn that police in Azusa have arrested Fernando Porras, 43, for allegedly poisoning his wife's Rice Krispie's cereal. The suspected would be "cereal killer" was charged with attempted murder and ordered held in lieu of $1 million bail.

Oh Snap, Crackle and Pop!!!

CALIFORNIA: An LA county Sheriff's deputy was arrested for allegedly smuggling heroin hidden in a bean and cheese burrito into the courthouse lockup. The deputy, Henry Marin, 27, pleaded not guilty to bringing drugs into a jail.

BURP!

CALIFORNIA: A woman at a Burbank McDonald's restaurant offered another customer sex in exchange for his Chicken McNuggets. He declined the offer. It is not certain whether he didn't want to part with his McNuggets or that she was just too homely.

My gosh, how hungry was she?

CALIFORNIA: A California porn star, who is also a skydiving instructor may be in for trouble. The porno skydiver was recently seen in a YouTube video posted online showing him jumping out of an airplane and having sex with a lady skydiver in midair. Police are still trying to discover whether Alex Torres' sex dive broke any law.

Geronimo…

CALIFORNIA: Baron Stein, an unemployed San Diego tow truck driver, admitted he was struggling to feed his family when he stole 1,000 pounds of avocados, worth $1,500. He confessed his crime and took a plea deal. He was given no jail time but as part of his probation he was ordered to possess no more than 10 avocados at any one time.

Yuk, yuk…A Judge with a sense of humor…

CALIFORNIA: The fellow who, as a child, voiced the voice of the peanuts cartoon character, Charlie Brown, threatened to kill a

West coast plastic surgeon because he didn't like the breasts the doctor put on his ex-girlfriend. Peter Robbins, 57, voiced Charlie Brown in classic TV shows like the Christmas and "Great Pumpkin" specials for five years. Police report that Robbins left dozens of threatening handwritten screeds and voice messages for Dr. Lori Saltz.

ROBBINS – YOU ARE A BLOCKHEAD!

MONTANA: A would-be thief had a change of heart – as a clerk was handing him the money. The bandit broke down crying after demanding cash from a pizza restaurant – and sobbed that he only wanted to feed his family. The clerk was so moved, he offered to make the man a pizza and wings. The would-be thief took the meal and left. No arrest was made.

Nothing like good Christian kindness…

ARIZONA: A slick talking Arizona man has managed to escape from jails in two states by pretending to be other inmates. Rocky Delgado Marquez, 34, was arrested in 2010 on DWI forgery and other charges, but got away from an Arizona jail in May 2011 by convincing jailers he was a different inmate. He spent eight months on the lam and was arrested in Detroit. He was being held pending extradition, but allegedly escaped again last week using the same scam.

He sounds like the Galloping Ghost...

TEXAS: A lawmaker has proposed a law forcing all exotic dancers to be licensed – and to wear ID tags displaying their true names and license numbers while stripping. State Rep. Bill Zedler says he hopes the move will discourage women from entering the profession. It would at least guarantee that no "Amber" or "Aurora" or "Brandi" or "Chastity" or "Crystal" of "Destiny" or "Lola" mounts the pole in Texas again.

No chance this will ever pass – legislators love strip joints. We are certain that Amber, Aurora, Brandi, Chastity, Crystal, Destiny and Lola will be with us for a long time...

ARIZONA: A Phoenix couple seeking a divorce hit an unusual snag that could prevent the marriage from legally being dissolved. A judge is questioning whether a same sex marriage ban bars him from ending the union, because the husband was born a woman and underwent a sex change, but retained female reproductive organs and gave birth to three children. Judge Douglas Gerlach said in late June, that he was unable to find any legal authority defining a man as someone who can give birth. Gerlach has questioned whether Thomas and Nancy Beatie's union was a same sex marriage.

OMG! Where is the Wisdom of Solomon when we need it?

OREGON: A long-haired man in Portland was arrested for allegedly choking his girlfriend with his dreadlocks. Caleb Grotberg, 32, allegedly used his hair as a weapon. This proves that dreadlocks can't choke people, but that people with dreadlocks can choke people.

Hey Rasta man, you no choke yo' woman with dem dreads, neva…

NEVADA: During a recent screening of the movie "The Bourne Legacy" at a Sparks' movie theater, a patron accidently shot himself in the buttocks when his weapon, for unknown reasons, went off in his pocket. He slowly stood up, apologized to his fellow moviegoers and went to the hospital. We learn he was not arrested, because he had a permit to carry the gun.

Probably good the gun wasn't in his front pocket....

TEXAS: Houston polices are on the lookout for a crazed stalker who twice rammed his car into the front entrance of a local TV station, because he thought it would impress the traffic reporter. Jennifer Reyna of KPRC-TV had already taken out a restraining order on the man.

Hey, Love, love, love makes them do such foolish things...

NEVADA: A furious homeowner shot a golfer for slicing a golf ball through the homeowner's window near the 16th hole of a course in Reno. The golfer was not seriously injured, but we learn that the shooter will get more than a one stroke penalty. He is facing a felony assault rap.

You assume the risk of a broken window when you choose to live on a golf course, idiot!

NEVADA: A man who attempted an armed robbery in the parking lot of a Las Vegas restaurant decided he had better get rid of the gun after the intended victims drove off. Expecting the law to arrive at any second, he tried to convince a waitress to hold the gun for him. Either the suspect or the waitress – police are not certain which – threw the gun into a deep fryer. The deep-fried gun exploded, but no one was hurt.

Hiding a gun in a deep fryer is the craziest idea since paintball.

ARIZONA: Mexican drug smugglers used powerful pneumatic cannon to propel more than 30 cans, each packed with 85 pounds of marijuana, over a border fence and into Arizona. "We've seen catapults but nothing like this," said Border Patrol spokesman Kyle Estes who said the Mary Jane was worth an estimated $42,000.

The headline to the story simply read: "POT SHOT."

NEW MEXICO: We discovered that Eastern New Mexico University recently received 80 rolls of toilet tissue along with an unsigned note from a person claiming to be a recent graduate apologizing for his ripping off that much tissue during his undergraduate days. The writer further admitted to have undergone a renewed dedication to Christianity and felt guilty about the petty "potty" theft.

He must have TP'ed every house in Eastern New Mexico…

COLORADO: They say "be careful what you steal." A wildlife educator briefly parked his van while heading to a school in the town of Englewood. A thief grabbed the van, not knowing its passengers included a 13 foot python, a rattlesnake, three scorpions and a tarantula.

YIKES!!!!

CALIFORNIA: A parent in the town of Albany was so angry when she found her son received a C plus grade in in his chemistry class, that she filed a lawsuit against his teacher. The mother maintains that her son really did "A" level work and that the teacher gave him a C plus in a deliberate effort to ruin his future. The case is pending.

Sorry mom, you won't win this silly lawsuit....

CALIFORNIA: Northern California farmers are “shell-shocked” over a crook stealing 80,000 pounds of walnuts from a freight company. The nuts, packed into two tractor trailers, are worth about $300,000.

We've learned that police are working hard to “Crack” the case! Yuk, yuk, yuk...

CALIFORNIA: A fleeing robber was arrested in Los Angeles after he jumped a fence at a baseball field and ran into several dozen police officers who were handing out Christmas toys to underprivileged children at the ball field.

Idiot!

CALIFORNIA: We learn that thugs in Oakland attacked a newsman and a camera man for a local CBS affiliate, while the journalists were doing a live TV report outside a high school. The thieves made off with a $10,000 high definition camera, roughed up the camera man and fled in a Mercedes Benz. The camera man was slightly injured, but is now back to work.

Fled in a Mercedes – must have been high class thugs!

CALIFORNIA: A disabled grandmother, armed only with bear spray, told police she fended off 13 intruders who were after the medical marijuana she had growing in her back yard. The woman grabbed the spray and emptied the can on the would be thieves.

Pssssst Psssssssssstt Psssssssssssssttt.....

CALIFORNIA: An 82 year old woman was arrested for allegedly committing five burglaries, in which she stole a total of $17,000 cash from El Segundo area doctors' offices. A frail Doris Gamble, who has been pulling burglaries since 1955 wore a hearing aid as a judge ordered her held in lieu of $250,000 bail.

Doris you are now too old for these kind of heists!

CALIFORNIA: A food plant worker died on the job after being cooked to death in an oven. Authorities are investigating the death of a 62 year old worker, whose body was found in a Bumble Bee Tuna plant in Santa Fe Springs. It is unclear how the six year employee ended in the industrial steamer, but officials say it was probably a freak accident.

Ya' think!

CALIFORNIA: Lorenzo Oliver, 54, was arrested and taken to jail for attacking an opossum in his back yard, after the possum went after his dogs. Oliver has now been cleared of all charges and he has also been cleared to sue the Anaheim Police Department – because it is not against the law to kill opossums in California.

Can we say the police jumped the gun?

CHAPTER TWO

WEIRD CRIMINAL LAW STORIES FROM NEW YORK, NEW ENGLAND AND THE EAST COAST

NEW YORK: A Long Island hooker sold more than just sausages at her roadside hot dog truck. According to police sources, she used her truck to also peddle her own flesh, even though she had been arrested on the same charge eight years before. Catherine Scalia, 45, was arrested recently when she offered an undercover officer an off menu special and took him back to her East Rockaway house for some home cooking. The mother of four pleaded not guilty to a prostitution charge and was held on $2,000 bail.

That's some "hot Dog" wagon...

NEW JERSEY: Two sisters in their 90's drove off a 27 year old carjacker. The women who had been shopping in Hamilton Township had just stepped into their car when the would be bandit sprang from the back seat brandishing a knife. The 94 year old driver threw her arm back and slugged him while her 93 year old sister began screaming. He ran off but was soon captured.

What a wuss…

NEW YORK CITY: It has been reported that police aren't safe to leave their bicycles unlocked in the city. A bike patrol officer found that out the hard way when a criminal swiped his bike outside a Brooklyn store. Tommy Kwan, owner of a furniture store, said the officer left his bike unattended when he popped in to say hello around 3 pm. "When he went to leave, the bike was gone," Kwan said. The bike was clearly marked with the letters "NYPD." To add insult to injury the officer also lost his book of blank summonses.

Sounds like Officer Doofuss…

PENNSYLVANIA: Kenneth Butterworth, a motorist in Philly, was upset about a driver who he believed had cut him off. So, he allegedly pulled out a medieval crossbow and pointed it at the other motorist. It is reported that no one was hurt. Butterworth had no arrows with him.

So, where is Robin Hood whey you need him?

MARYLAND: Recently, the Frederick County Courthouse was evacuated after someone reported a suspicious package. The package turned out to be a coconut. The coconut was taken into custody after it was inspected by the bomb squad. We do not know why the coconut turned up at the courthouse.

Whoo Hoo! Pina Coladas for everyone!

DISTRICT OF COLUMBIA: We learn that a congressman's Twitter account was hacked. A cyber vandal broke into the account of freshman Representative Bill Johnson (R-Ohio), replacing his photo with an image of a nude man. Capitol Police, House of

Representatives security and Twitter have all launched investigations of the matter.

Where was former Representative Anthony Wiener when this happened?

DISTRICT OF COLUMBIA: A Washington, DC area school has officially charged a mother and father for making their three young children late for school. Amy and Marc Denicore are facing three misdemeanor charges, each carrying a $500 fine. Their children ages 6, 7 and 9 have been late nearly thirty times between September and January, usually by less than three minutes. The Denicores maintain no matter what the school alleges, they believe they have not committed a crime. It is not clear whether the school officials realize that both the parents are trained lawyers.

Let those mean old school officials try to get three little kids to school on time every day....N-sane!

VERMONT: State troopers in this state were very embarrassed after they learned a prisoner who painted the state seal on the doors of three dozen state police cars secretly included the image of a pig in the design. The pig wasn't discovered until one day a trooper took a good look at the seal and he realized that he had been driving around with a bogus seal.

Yuk, Yuk, Yuk....Pigs! What a sense of humor that prison painter had!

MASSACHUSETTS: This must have been one heckuva basketball game. The winning and losing coaches of sixth grade basketball teams in Springfield got into a postgame fight. The fight ended when the assistant coach on the losing team bit off part of the winning coach's ear.

...Sounds more like Mike Tyson.

MASSACHUSETTS: A Fall River dentist has been arrested for finding a new and bizarre use for paper clips. Michael Clair pleaded guilty to a variety of fraud related charges after using paper clips instead of far more expensive stainless steel rods as the posts in root canal procedures.

The crime of the century, no?

MASSACHUSETTS: An employee at the Groton water Department was spending his time working on another liquid than water. Plant officials said that he had been operating a still and making moonshine liquor at the plant. No word on whether he was fired and arrested or just fired.

Get you a copper kettle and get you a copper coil and just watch them jugs a fill'n in the pale moonlight!

NEW YORK CITY: A 400 pound felon claims in a law suit against the Corrections Department that he spent eight months in jail in one set of street clothes, because the city wouldn't find jail clothes that fit him. Elias Diaz, 55, claims that he was humiliated because he wears a size 7X. Correction officials only stock jail clothing up to size

6X. He is asking for $1million in his suit filed in federal court.

He doesn't have a "fat" chance of winning this one!

NEW YORK: An Amish youth in western New York State was arrested for alleged drunk driving. He was in his horse and buggy. According to a police report the youth was clopping along in his horse drawn buggy when a police officer spotted an open can of beer in the buggy. Deputies accused Lewis Hostetler, 17, of DWI, rowdiness, and resisting arrest.

All in a horse and buggy? This one will never hold up in court....

NEW JERSEY: It has been reported that a South Jersey woman allegedly climbed over the counter of a Cumberland County convenience store and attacked a clerk when she learned that there were no cooked sausages ready to buy. Brittany Glanville, 25, was charged with disorderly conduct.

Yep. They should be hot and ready to take out!!!

MARYLAND: Timothy Randall Clark picked the worst day to do his Christmas shoplifting. He was charged with attempting to steal more than $400 worth of video games from a Charles County Walmart on "Shop with a Cop Day," a local charity event. When security guards caught Clark allegedly sticking the games under his shirt they didn't have to look far for a cop, because they were all over.

What an imbecile!

NEW JERSEY: Daniel Collins, Jr., 72, was accused of pointing a revolver at his 47 year old neighbor in their Teaneck apartment building. The victim passed gas very loudly as he walked past Collins' apartment. It was loud enough to hear through the closed apartment door and Collins allegedly emerged brandishing the firearm. Collins held his fire and later was freed on bail.

Oh Poot!

NEW JERSEY: A bank teller in Mount Holly was arrested for allegedly ripping off $100,000 from a customer by creating a fraudulent debit card linked to the customer's account. The victim customer notified police. When police investigated, they found that this victim's account included about $500,000 he got by allegedly filing fraudulent tax returns.

They are both going to jail. Put them both in the same cell – they deserve each other!

PENNSYLVANIA: They say times are tough in Scranton. As a matter of fact, times are so tough that Mayor Chris Doherty unilaterally cut the pay of all city employees, including his own, to the state's minimum wage of $7.25 an hour. The Mayor said the city is out of money. We understand that municipal unions are taking Doherty to court.

Minimum wage is better than no wage!

PENNSYLVANIA: A man in the town of Washington allegedly broke into a fast food place and stole nine bags of potato chips. He then ate them along his route – leaving an easy trail of chips and bags for police to follow. Yes, he was caught.

Do not let the chips fall where they may....

CONNECTICUT: Mike Apatow, an off duty firefighter, was pulled over by police in Milford. The police had used a radiation detecting anti- terror device. No arrest was made on possible terrorism charges once Apatow explained that he was undergoing medical tests that required injections of small doses of radiation to track blood flow.

ALLAH AKBAR!

PENNSYLVANIA: A suspected shoplifter fled topless from security officers. Aishana Clayton, 26, was nabbed at a Pathmark in suburban Philly. As Clayton was led to a security office she began to punch, bite and scratch at officers who grabbed her shirt, but she tore free and fled from the store to her auto. “Her breasts were swinging as she ran to the car," Upper Darby police superintendent Michael Chitwood said. She remains at large

Security officers were lucky not have gotten a bust in the mouth...

NEW YORK: A group of Syracuse teenagers who ate at a local restaurant almost pulled off what is called a "dine and dash." Where you eat and run before paying the bill. Their escape failed when they ran to their car outside the restaurant, only to discover that they had locked the car keys inside. A girl in the group went to a nearby police station asking for help with retrieving the keys just as the restaurant owner was calling the same police station.

Dimwits....

PENNSYLVANIA: A man in Peters Township left his bag of marijuana and hallucinogenic mushrooms at a local grocery store. A customer found it and turned it over to a clerk, who called police. When the dope head called the store to ask about his bag he was told to go to the police station. So he did…

Yes, we know the end of the story, he was an idiot…

DISTRICT OF COLUMBIA: A bicycling crime fighter got his stolen bike back after he spotted the stolen Cannondale on Craigslist. He made an appointment to meet the thief to buy it. Danny Lesh of Washington convinced the bike bandit to let him take a test ride – and he simply rode home with the bike. The thief actually called him and threatened to call the police, which made Lesh laugh.

Turnabout is fair play in the game of bike theft…

PENNSYLVANIA: A former state trooper is in trouble but happy that he only got house arrest and probation. Why? Douglas Sversko, 44, received the above mentioned sentence for sending a video of himself dancing in the nude to a 13-year-old girl he had met on line. The problem was there was no 13-year-old girl. Instead, he sent his video to a male police investigator posing on line as a 13-year-old girl.

Freaky fool…

PENNSYLVANIA: A would be crook was arrested in Lancaster County after he tried to buy goods at a convenience store with a stolen credit card and the clerk recognized him. Also, the stolen card belonged to the clerk's mother.

Dumkopf!

PENNSYLVANIA: A 300 pound man left security personnel at a Philly area Walmart dumbfounded when he walked into the store "buck-naked" and proceeded to shoplift a pair of socks. Police confronted him at the door and Tasered him when he ignored their command to stop.

Perhaps he thought he was invisible….

PENNSYLVANIA: A good citizen read about a robbery in Leechburg and thought he recognized the bandit. It was himself! Timothy, who maintains to have split personalities, told police that one of them was the crook who had held up the local restaurant. So he turned himself in.

At least a part of him was law abiding.

PENNSYLVANIA: A couple in this state has been accused of trying to blow up a rival couple's car by stuffing flaming tampons down the gas tank. Patricia and Quentin Deshong didn't succeed in blowing up the 2006 Ford Fusion, but they did cause serious damage, according to police.

Flaming tampons... Why???

PENNSYLVANIA: Well, at least we know the motive for the crime! A 49 year old toothless woman has confessed to robbing a bank in Carmichaels. She told police she wanted to use the stolen money to buy a set of dentures.

The headline read: "She Wanted to Put Her Money Where her Mouth is."

PENNSYLVANIA: How is this for stupid? Keith Rebori held up a Poconos pharmacy and left behind a great clue used to track him down – his birth certificate. Rebori, 23, held up the East Stroudsburg CVS pharmacy for painkillers on Thanksgiving of 2011. Nearby, police found a hooded sweatshirt used in the hold up and a backpack containing his birth certificate.

DUMMY!

NEW YORK: They called him the "Ty-D-Bol Bandit." Why? A robber attempted to hold up three banks in the city of Utica armed only with a toilet bowl plunger. The bandit quickly learned that the plunger did not strike fear in the hearts of bank tellers. The police report stated that he was soon captured and sent to jail.

In other words he was flushed!

MASSACHUSETTS: A would be burglar in Brocton came upon a home whose garage door had a small gap from the floor. The burglar tried to squeeze under the garage door and got his head trapped in the gap. He could not get into the garage or out of the garage. The thief was stuck with the door on his ear for nine hours until he was discovered, rescued and arrested.

M B SILL!

MASSACHUSETTS: Using profanity in public could now cost you a $20 fine in the town of Middleborough. Residents voted 183 to 50, in favor of a police proposal aimed at loud, profanity spewing teenagers who often gather in the town's public park.

Soon of a #%&%...GOD !$%&*##x... Bull x#@%$&...

MASSACHUSETTS: A Boston area idiot telephoned 911 to complain that a deli had failed to put mayonnaise on his sandwich. “So don’t buy it!” the operator shouted at the man and threatened to have him arrested. As it turns out it was reported that the man was not drunk, only very stupid.

D’OH…

MASSACHUSETTS: A bicyclist in Holbrook said he was robbed and beaten by a man swinging stolen sausage links and then a wrench. Police report a Good Samaritan jogger found the cyclist yelling for help, and saw Michael Baker, 22, take off with the victim’s bike, police report. Baker was soon arrested.

Arrested for assault with a dangerous weapon: stolen sausage links!!

MASSACHUSETTS: A man in Lowell was charged with assault with a dangerous weapon after he tossed French fries at his 11 year old stepdaughter. She wasn’t hurt and he was freed without bail.

And now for another arrest for assault with a dangerous weapon: French fries!!!

CHAPTER THREE

WEIRD CRIMINAL LAW STORIES FROM THE GREAT MIDWEST

ILLINOIS: A burglar in Galesburg broke into a house, but didn't take any cash, jewelry or other valuables. Instead, he stole only a bag of kinky sex toys near the bed of the victim – who happened to be a sex toy saleswoman, who was away at a convention in Las Vegas.

BBBBZZZZZZZZZZZZZZ...

OHIO: A woman in the town of Hamilton was arrested for trying to sneak into the local jail. Deputies spotted her climbing over a barbed wire fence and into the rear yard of the lockup. When they ordered her to leave she asked them to arrest her. The deputies were pleased to oblige.

Her lover was probably on the inside....

MICHIGAN: An allegedly drunken man strayed into the wrong home and got into bed with the couple who lived there. The pair fled and called police. Police said, when the 27 year old intruder woke up he murmured, "This isn't my house!" The man, a neighbor who lived a few doors down, was arrested for suspicion of illegal entry.

Another drunken dummy!

NORTH DAKOTA: A Bismarck athlete got a good scare when a naked man leaped out of bushes and started to chase her. The 30 year old runner put on the speed as her pursuer held his genitals and made lewd remarks, but finally gave up the chase. Police are looking for the man.

Ana now we have running perverts....

NORTH DAKOTA: The mayor of the Old West town of Medora is sticking his neck out – literally; he is volunteering to be hanged. Of course, it would be all for show. Doug Ellison wants to erect a gallows and put on a show for tourists: He would gun someone down, have a trial and then get the ultimate punishment – a hanging. The performance would take only 20 minutes he said, because "anything longer than that and the tourists would lose interest."

True that. But still it's a horrible idea!!

KANSAS: A fugitive on the lam in Topeka, burst into a home where a frightened couple fed him and promised him money if he would leave. The couple fled the home when the fugitive fell asleep. Thereafter he was quickly arrested. He then filed a "breach of oral contract" suit against the couple, because they never paid him. He is seeking damages of $235,000.

What a knucklehead!

KANSAS: A co-ed from Olathe found nearly $400 worth of cocaine in a used book that she bought online. Sophia Stockton, fearing the white powder was anthrax, took it to police. An officer "came back and said, "You didn't happen to order some cocaine with your textbook?'" she recalled. She suspects the drug was left in the book by a previous owner.

Or maybe the tooth fairy put it there for her....

MINNESOTA: A man was arrested for allegedly stealing Freon from a neighbor's air conditioner and inhaling the refrigerant. Brentyn Krueger, 36, was found slumped over his neighbor's outdoor air conditioner unit, according to the police report.

Can we say it was a "cool" arrest?

MINNESOTA: A suburban Minneapolis man managed to walk out of a store with a 19 inch TV shoved down his pants. He also had a remote control for the TV, power cords and a bottle of brake fluid in his pants. Eric Lee King, 21, was caught when a police officer saw him drop a box of candy in the parking lot. The officer realized that King was walking strangely and at the same time he was trying to hold up his pants.

Those must have been some really big pants!

MINNESOTA: Here's one about another easy arrest. Arden Hills police did not have much trouble arresting a drunken man after he drove his car up to the gasoline pump at police headquarters and tried filling his tank. One officer said, "It's humorous that someone would be arrested for DWI at police headquarters."

...Safest place for a DWI arrest, no?

NEBRASKA: Yep, a Nebraska thief picked the wrong car stereo to steal. He took a Lincoln man's one of a kind sound system and was arrested when he went to a sound shop to have the stolen equipment installed in his own car. As it turned out the manager of the shop was the victim of the theft.

Ironic, yes?

IOWA: A Des Moines woman was so angry about being defriended on Facebook, she went to the ex-friend's home and allegedly burned down her garage. It appears that Jennifer Harris was angry that her target tried to organize a party for her on Facebook and no one wanted to come. Police report that the dispute escalated to defriending and then to arson.

The next step may have been murder if an arrest hadn't been made!

WISCONSIN: My gosh, how bad was this date? A man and his girlfriend got into an argument during the ride home from a night out in Madison. The argument got so bad the man decided to jump out of their car to get away from her. Problem was, the car was still moving at 25 mph. The man hit the pavement hard, suffering a head injury.

We hope these two don't have kids together…

OHIO: A marijuana dealer in Cincinnati had a quite unique security system for his stash. Alligators! Accused marijuana grower Lavon

McCants allegedly had two gators, each measuring 4 feet long, stationed to protect cannabis plants. Police charged McCants with drug possession and illegally keeping exotic animals.

Two four foot long gators are not very dangerous.

SOUTH DAKOTA: A 28-year-old prison inmate has filed a federal lawsuit against the hospital that circumcised him as a newborn. In his suit, Dean Cochrun alleges that the procedure "robbed" him of his sexual prowess. Cochrun who is locked up for kidnapping is seeking damages of $1,000 from the hospital and he would also like to have his foreskin restored.

We've heard of some silly lawsuits, but this one won't "stand up." Yuk, yuk, yuk...

MINNESOTA: A waitress at a diner was thrilled when someone left her a $12,000 tip after a meal. Her joy did not last long. Police seized the money, because they said it smelled like marijuana and must have been left by drug dealers. The waitress, who thought she was doing the right thing by reporting the big tip to police, is suing to get the money back.

Police are always quick to confiscate what they believe to be drug money because they can use the money for their department – they know criminals never come back for the money!

INDIANA: James Henderson, 28, of Valparaiso was hospitalized after police found him unconscious on a road. His blood alcohol level was measured at a whopping 0.552 percent. It is not unusual for people who have an above 0.4 blood alcohol level to fall into a coma. Not so with Henderson. It is reported that he appears to be on the mend.

Bet he has one whale of a headache though...

INDIANA: A week after the above story was reported James Henderson, 28, of Valparaiso was again found sprawled on a street with a blood alcohol level of 0.297. This is, of course, an improvement over the last time he was found passed out with that 0.552 blood alcohol level.

At least Henderson is drinking less...

IOWA: This guy was arrested for disorderly conduct. Why? Angered at receiving a parking ticket, Derick Thoene went into the City Hall in Iowa City and allegedly told a receptionist: "I have your parking attendant in the trunk of my car. Do you want him dead or alive?" That's why he was arrested.

Disorderly indeed!

OHIO: This is a weird one. A speeding motorist missed a turn and crashed into a house in Rossford. Then it got really weird. The man in the car jumped out of his car, stripped naked and chased the woman homeowner, police say. A Marine who lives in the neighborhood restrained the naked driver until police arrived to make an arrest.

Cuckoo Cuckoo Cuckoo....

MICHIGAN: A suburban Detroit man has filed a class action lawsuit against his local AMC movie theater, complaining that it charges too much for concession snacks. We learn further that the company has declined to comment.

Yeah, that's right and the rent is too damn high!

OHIO: How about this one? We learn that one incident has resulted in the suspension of the police chief of Mount Sterling and the disbanding of his entire force. The incident involved a village police officer using a Taser on a nine year old boy, who neighbors said is big for his age. Madison County sheriff's deputies are now taking over all the police duties in Mount Sterling, while the incident is being investigated.

Just how big was this nine year old?

OHIO: Recently, an elementary school in Canfield was forced into lock-down after a mother showed up at school dressed in a

Mickey Mouse costume to surprise her child on Valentine's Day. The woman had followed school rules by signing in at the front desk to gain entry. However, she then went into the ladies room and emerged in costume. School staffers who thought she was deranged called the police. No arrest was made.

What! No law against dressing up as Mickey Mouse during school hours?

OHIO: No courtroom sketch artist for this trial! A TV station in Cleveland has started a courtroom puppet show. WOIO is using Muppet-like puppets to illustrate a local official's corruption trial because the federal court does not allow cameras inside. The re-enactments included puppet versions of the judge, the defendant, jurors and witnesses reciting lines directly from the day's court transcripts.

This is about the silliest thing I've ever heard of...

OHIO: In Athens, the local police chief wound up on his own police blotter after sheriff's deputies conducted what is called a "buy-and-bust" drug sting at his home. Chief Kelsey Lanning is now in the county jail. The situation is very awkward for the chief's underling officers.

We are sure he was only buying the dope for medicinal purposes...

OKLAHOMA: Talk about irony! A ninth grader at Mustang High School got in trouble after discovering his substitute teacher sleeping in class. He took a photograph of her and showed it to school authorities. Instead, of thanking the youngster for exposing the sleepy substitute, school authorities suspended him for using a cell phone in school.

Kids just can't catch a break in school anymore...

MISSOURI: A woman was arrested after she attacked her 21 year old son's heroin dealer with a baseball bat. Sherrie Gavan, who is 4 foot 11 and weighs 115 pounds, allegedly struck the dealer on both his arms after confronting him at his home. We learn that despite her brave stand against drugs, she still faces assault charges.

Batter up.....

MISSOURI: A St. Louis man was shot and killed while trying to circulate a petition promoting a ballot initiative called "A Safer Missouri." It is still undetermined why Darryl Winston, 55, was gunned down, but witnesses saw him arguing with a man before he was shot.

Isn't it apparent that he was shot because he had pissed off the criminals?

MISSOURI: We learn that the city of St. Louis has a big school bus mystery. Since the start of the 2011-12 school year five full sized yellow buses have gone missing without a trace. No one knows whether they have been misplaced or stolen. "Why would you take a school bus, and where do you hide a school bus?" asked a local police official.

Chop shop...

MISSOURI: A gubernatorial candidate in St. Louis who had been touting his economics degree was unmasked as a liar when a local newspaper discovered he had left out the word "home" in "home economics" degree. David Spence claimed to be an economics major in his campaign fliers and on his Website. He maintains that the controversy was "overblown."

Liar, liar pants on fire...

INDIANA: Clinton Edwards, 27, was shot in the leg while trying to burglarize a home in rural Indiana. He didn't let a little blood stop him though. After fleeing the scene of that burglary he fled across the county line and despite his wound allegedly pulled another burglary. He was caught and arrested shortly after this second burglary.

Determination....

INDIANA: A handcuffed drug suspect stole a small Indiana town's only police car – then radioed in to the police station to ask where the vehicle's cigarette lighter was located. William F. Blankenship, 22, allegedly stole the car on a Thursday which was found a few days later. The vehicle had been wrecked and submerged in water authorities said. Blankenship is still missing.

Did the police drag the water for his body?

ILLINOIS: A four year old Chicago girl was listed as in good condition after she was wounded in the ankle while jumping on a bed where a handgun had been stashed under the mattress. An adult, Jarquise Upton, was charged with one felony count of unlawful use of a weapon. We have not learned her relationship to the child.

Are our children safe anywhere anymore? Bang! Pow! Boom!

ILLINOIS: An orchestra was performing Brahms's Symphony No. 2 when the real action got started in the audience. Two concert goers at the Chicago Symphony added some unexpected hockey like fisticuffs to the usually refined affair. A man in his 30's punched out a 67 year old man in a fight over seats. The younger man who threw the first punch took off before police arrived.

...And the band played on!

ILLINOIS: We learn that a legislator has introduced a bill that would ban texting while riding a bicycle. The bill's sponsor says she wrote the legislation after getting a ton of complaints from constituents who think that two wheeled texting is a prevalent problem.

Yes, about as prevalent as a fish riding a bicycle.

ILLINOIS: Ambitious thieves in Chicago have stolen an entire building. Scrap metal bandits took an abandoned steel structure after telling neighbors it had been scheduled for demolition. When the owner was told the building was gone he could not believe it.

Gone with the wind...

ILLINOIS: According to police, an Illinois woman robbing a bank brought along her five year old son. Lauri Ruble was charged with armed robbery of the Wauconda Community Bank while clutching her son in one hand and a butcher knife in the other hand. Ruble got away with $4,800, police report. However, she was arrested and faces criminal charges, while also being investigated by the Department of Children and Family Services.

Are they going to charge the kid as an aider and abettor?

ILLINOIS: An injured Chicago woman has won the right to sue a dead man after his severed leg hit her. The woman can pursue a claim against the estate of Hiroyuki Joho, 18, who walked in front of a train in 2008 and was killed. His dismembered leg went flying onto the platform and struck Gayane Zokhrabov. An appeals court ruled that she could sue, because he was responsible for getting in the train's path.

Boy, that is one grim story…

OHIO: A report out of Toledo maintains that an armed man dressed up like Darth Vader robbed a bank carrying a handgun. The robber escaped on a BMX bicycle, according to police.

The robber may have told the teller, "Luke, I am your father..."

OHIO: They say that a woman has devised a new and creative business model for her maid service – just break into a person's home and start cleaning. "Cleaning Fairy" Sue Warren allegedly broke into a home, washed dishes, and vacuumed, and then left a bill behind for $75. Of course, she left her contact information on the bill and demanded payment when the baffled victim telephoned to ask what had happened.

COOOKCOO.....COOOKCOO.....

MICHIGAN: A boxer recently received some good news and some bad news. Martin Tucker won his latest bout but, was quickly arrested for a credit union robbery in the town of Temperance. His opponent had punched Tucker in the nose and FBI agents, who already suspected him, got hold of a Q-tip Tucker used to stop the bleeding. Tucker's DNA matched genetic evidence found on the steering wheel of the getaway car.

Schmuck!

MICHIGAN: Authorities in Michigan have devised a most creative way to warn about drinking and driving – talking urinal cakes. The state Licensed Beverage Association has distributed the electronic devices to numerous bars. As drinkers use the restroom the device plays recorded warning encouraging drunks to call a taxi.

The next bright idea will be commodes that sing opera…

ILLINOIS: Shannon White, 36, called 911 six times, upset that her boyfriend refused to serve her any more beer, according to Belleville police. She was arrested for disorderly conduct and false use of 911 emergency service lines.

….More beer…HIC-CUP…

ILLINOIS: We learn that taxi passengers in Chicago may now have to pay to vomit. Starting July 1, 2012, cabbies have been allowed to add a special "upchuck charge" to the fares of customers who vomit in the back of the cab. The charge is $50 per puke.

Raaaaaaallllllfffff....

OHIO: A Cincinnati man who has an unhealthy fascination with teddy bears has been arrested for the fourth time by police for allegedly fornicating with a teddy bear in public. He was caught in "flagrante delicto" with the teddy bear near a health clinic.

Sounds like he is in need of a mental health clinic.

ILLINOIS: Police arrested two women for flashing their breasts at male golfers at the Woodlands Golf Course in the city of Alton. Shelly Lewis, 45, and Alicia Binford, 41, did not have any clubs with them when police arrested them for showing off their bare tops.

They both sound a little too old for this kind of stunt!

MICHIGAN: A public works employee thought he was being responsible when he turned a gun over to police after he found it while he was mowing grass on a roadside. Authorities from Wayne County thought otherwise and fired him for possessing a weapon while on duty. The worker, John Chevilott, was just two years from retirement.

This is so bogus. Where is the NRA when you really need 'em?

OHIO: If prisoners at the Summit County Jail want to get their one phone call, they had better know how to get down and dance. Why? A guard at the facility was fired after he forced inmates to dance to the Usher song "Yeah!" before they made calls.

"No!"

ILLINOIS: A thief in Chicago was ratted out by his loot. He held up a Radio Shack and grabbed electronics – including a GPS. We learn that it was easy for police to nab him because of the GPS. He was on the lam for only two hours.

Dunce! You do not go on the lam with a GPS!

ILLINOIS: Another dumb criminal in Chicago pulled the following caper. She went into a bank and passed a note to the teller demanding money. The teller was polite. She advised her the bank was closed and that she should come back the next day. The would be bandit walked out, but was arrested soon after her photo showed up on surveillance footage.

Nope….just not very bright…

INDIANA: Chadwyck Voegeli, 20, of Fort Wayne pretended to be a police officer. It is reported that he used his "tricked out" cellphone that was flashing red and blue lights to pull over car. Unfortunately for him the car he had targeted was carrying two off duty police officers, according to the police report. Voegeli allegedly sped off, ditched his car and ran through a bar before police captured him.

Nothing worse than those wannabe cops…

MINNESOTA: We learn that lawyers at the firm of Milavetz, Gallop & Milavetz are suing Wells Fargo Bank, claiming the bank should have stopped the lawyers from paying

$400,000 to a Nigerian fraud ring. The Nigerian fraudsters sent the firm an email three years ago, claiming to be a Korean woman needing an advance to collect a legal settlement.

Suckers…

ILLINOIS: Here's a strange and sad story. A swan attacked Anthony Hensley, a kayaker at a Chicago condominium complex. Initially, the swan capsized the kayak, then as final act, the swan kept Hensley from reaching the shore. It has been reported that the 37 year old Hensley drowned as a result of the swan attack.

Death by swan! How ignoble…

ILLINOIS: It's only news when… A woman was arrested for being drunk and disorderly and for biting her bull dog in the town of Lake in the Hills. The dog bit her back, but police decided that it was self defense. "The dog was not charged," said Police Sgt. Mark Smith. The woman was charged.

Chomp Chomp….

OKLAHOMA: They say a woman is asking herself if jail time was worth $14. The woman is facing jail time after she telephoned the local electric company and threatened to blow up its office after she was sent a $14 bill. In her own defense, she said that she was angry because she doesn't use that much power and she is having trouble paying her $40 a month rent.

Wow! The cost of living in Oklahoma sounds cheap.

ILLINOIS: A would be bank robber in Chicago needs to get his priorities straight. The man walked in the bank and ordered a teller to fill a bag with cash. The teller then handed the man the bag and the robber took off – but left the satchel of money behind. No arrest has been made.

What an absentminded nitwit…

OHIO: An Akron woman has been panhandling in her bikini on the streets of the town holding a sign reading, "I'm not homeless. I need boobs." Chrissy lance, 37, says she's begging for enough money to finance breast augmentation surgery (transplants) to enhance both her chest and her self-esteem.

She sounds like a boob!

KANSAS: An Overland Park man drove away from Harrah's Casino after a winning night of gambling and was followed by a woman in a gold colored sedan. The woman rear-ended the driver and then, as they exchanged information, the woman hit him with an electrical power strip. The man suffered cuts, but managed to get back in his car and flee. Authorities were able to identify the woman from casino surveillance cameras. She was promptly arrested. Assault and battery and attempted robbery we surmise.

THIS CHICK WAS A REAL LIVE PREDATOR. MEN BEWARE!

OHIO: An Ohio schoolteacher maintains her bosses discriminated against her – because she has a fear of children. Maria Waltherr-Willard, 61, asked not to have to educate young children, but was transferred from a high school to a junior high anyway. The veteran French and Spanish teacher sued the district after she was moved.

It won't take a lot of time for the court to dismiss such a silly lawsuit!

MISSOURI: The headline read, "Who needs a job when all you need are paychecks?" We learn that Victoria Calbert, 40, of Springfield was arrested for allegedly forging payroll checks and cashing them at Walmarts in Arkansas, Illinois, Iowa, Kansas, Oklahoma and Missouri. Walmart reports the 515 forged checks totaled $116,295.99. Calbert is unemployed.

Sounds like she paid herself a pretty good annual salary...

NEBRASKA: We learn that a man was arrested in Lincoln for arriving at a funeral home and allegedly posing as an undertaker in an effort to take two engagement rings from the fingers of his deceased fiancée. Terry Kurtzhals, 58, allegedly wore a name tag identifying himself as a funeral director and said he was representing the deceased's family. The funeral home's skeptical owner called police when Kurtzhals became agitated amid questioning.

What a cheap creep…

MISSOURI: How about this one? A St. Louis area man pleaded guilty to a murder conspiracy plot that would have framed a house cat for the crime. Brett Nash plotted to kill his wife's lover by having a hit man break into the paramour's home, electrocute him with a radio in the bathtub and then throw the man's cat into the water to make police believe that it was a tragic accident.

Such a crazy plot wouldn't work – too many working parts!!

MICHIGAN: A bank robbery suspect was arrested at a Southfield strip club after he allegedly hung red dye coated bills on the strippers' G-strings, and the manager called the police. Sometimes in bank robberies, tellers hand over cash stacks with exploding dye packs that spew red ink on the cash and the robber.

Dummy…

WISCONSIN: A 30-year-old man was arrested for selling marijuana as he rode around town on his unicycle. Police spotted the agile dealer pulling marijuana packets from his shorts and exchanging them for cash.

The headline read: He was a real dope "peddler."

WISCONSIN: Judge Tim Boyle of Racine ordered a father of nine who owes $90,000 in child support and interest to stop "breeding," until he can pay up. Judge Boyle sentenced Corey Curtis to probation in return for the deadbeat dad's agreement to accept the rare punishment. The judge further ruled if the number of Curtis' offspring goes into double digits, the deal would be off.

The headline read: "No Kidding."

IOWA: A jewelry store in North Liberty is offering free rifles to men who spend at least $1,999, for a diamond engagement ring. Jeweler Harold van Beck said he wants to "do something for the boy who doesn't like to hunt for diamonds but likes to hunt for deer."

They do love to cling to their guns and their religion...

IOWA: An Iowa City court has ruled that a dentist had the right to fire a woman for whom he felt an "irresistible attraction," because his feelings for her were negatively impacting his marriage. The court noted that the woman had been perfectly competent and had never flirted with him. The court further ruled that extracting her from his office might have been unfair – but it was perfectly legal.

What a dummy dentist. If he had an irresistible attraction to her he shouldn't have hired her in the first place ...

IOWA: A murder suspect dumped a glass of water over his attorney's head as the Cedar Rapids jury began deliberations. "It should have been a mistrial," shouted defendant Jerome Power before pouring the water on over Attorney Steve Addington's head. We learn that earlier in the trial Power held up a sign in the courtroom saying someone else committed the murder.

What a pinhead! A Guilty verdict will soon reveal itself...

INDIANA: A drunken driver smashed his car into a home in Indianapolis – but he tried to make up for it by asking the homeowners inside, "You want some pizza?" Police report that the driver had five beers with pals before getting in the vehicle while eating a slice. The rest of the pie was on the back seat. Luckily, no one was injured.

At least he remembered his manners...

KANSAS: A Wichita mugger stole a man's cellphone and wallet at gunpoint – before realizing him and his victim both had served time in the same prison. So he handed back the goods, shook his pal's hand and sent him on his way.

Honor among thieves???

ILLINOIS: Sarah Naughton, an assistant state's attorney in Cook County was drunk when she strolled into a lingerie shop called Taboo Tabou in Chicago. When she was asked to leave, Naughton, 31, became belligerent and bit a worker on the leg. We learn further that she has been placed on administrative leave from her job.

She sounds like one of those mad dog prosecutors!

ILLINOIS: Police in Chicago were amazed to find that a brazen drug farmer had planted two football fields worth of marijuana on the South Side of the city. It is reported that some of the 1,500 plants were the size of Christmas trees.

Yep, they're saying marijuana is becoming quite common...

ILLINOIS: It has been reported that two Naperville teens picked the wrong place to get high – in front of a police chief's home. Robert Pavelchik, who heads the police force in nearby Villa Park, was driving home when he noticed the two teens because he knew they didn't live on the block. He confronted them and discovered "they were blowing dope…right in front of my home. I smell the dope and I see the pipe and the bag of dope." Pavelchik held the two for local authorities.

It must have been 4:20...

CHAPTER FOUR

WEIRD CRIMINAL LAW STORIES FROM FLORIDA AND AROUND THE SOUTH

FLORIDA: A man stole a judge's office door name plate and posted a photo of himself with it on his girlfriend's Facebook page, police report. Steven Mulhall, 21, allegedly posted the photo showing him smirking while holding a name plate clearly showing the name "Judge Michael J. Orlando." It is not clear why he did this, but we did learn that he is a parolee who now faces a felony charge.

What an airhead...

FLORIDA: This was a funny report. It read, in part: "police arrested a man for bringing a pussy into a strip joint." Managers at the Emerald City gentlemen's club in the town of Murdock refused to allow Everett Lages, 47, and his pet kitten into the club. The intoxicated Lages became angry and telephoned 911. He was taken into custody for misuse of 911, trespassing and disorderly conduct. The kitten was put in the safe hands of animal control.

No pussies allowed in a strip joint – who knew?

FLORIDA: Authorities are searching for the former director of tourism in Okaloosa County, after he allegedly used county tax money to purchase a $710,000 yacht, and then went missing. County officials maintain they never realized he bought the boat until they received an invoice in the mail. They have no idea where he is or when he might return.

He's probably on his way to Paradise Island...

KENTUCKY: A man recently made amends for a theft he committed 54 years earlier. Bill Teitleff, 72, stole two hydrangeas bushes in May 1958 from Centennial Park in Nashville, Tennessee, because he did not have money for a Mother's Day gift. Teitleff, now a resident of Joy, Kentucky, said he always felt guilty about the theft. So for this Mother's Day he gave the park two plants from the root system of the original stolen bushes.

Another "Honest Abe."

TENNESSEE: A man who sired 21 children by eleven women is asking for the government's help in paying the child support after all the babies' mothers sued him at the same time. Desmond Hatchett, 33, told reporters, "I had four kids in the same year, twice." He later revealed he only had $400 to split among all the children and was promptly put in jail.

Sounds like Desmond needs a vasectomy...

NORTH CAROLINA: A 9 year old Gastonia boy was suspended from school for telling one of his friends that a teacher was cute. A substitute teacher overheard the remark and mentioned it to the principal, who punished the kid for "sexual harassment," according to the boy's mother.

This is so stupid! Where are we going as a society?

FLORIDA: A Port St. Lucie woman ended a night of heavy drinking by stabbing a male friend with a long and pointy mollusk shell. The incident was apparently so violent that police charged Patricia Wehr with aggravated battery with a deadly weapon for using a "seashell similar to a thick conch shell" to injure the man.

She should have just sold seashells by the seashore...

SOUTH CAROLINA: A lady in Aiken joked with a 10 year old on Halloween about stealing his trick or treat candy. The boy became so incensed that he pulled a gun on the lady. Fortunately, we learn the gun was not loaded.

What a little punk!!!

VIRGINIA: An allegedly drunken teenager was so out of control that his mother took him to the local police headquarters for help. Unfortunately, the teen charged at the police with a knife. It appears that the teenager went berserk, while with his mother in front of the Waynesboro Police Department headquarters. Police used stun guns to bring the kid under control. We learn further that the kid had wrecked his car earlier in the day.

He's going to grow up to be a real hell raiser...

NORTH CAROLINA: Do we know why a thief would break into jail? Such a situation might be achieved to practice his skills as a thief. A thief scaled the fence at a minimum security prison in Salisbury. Once inside he dismantled an air conditioner and walked away with its copper parts. He got away before guards could arrest him.

So he bested the "coppers" for the copper you say...

SOUTH CAROLINA: We learn that a man turned a Best Buy store into a big peep show. The high tech prankster managed to get control of the store's Wi-Fi, loading an image of a couple having sex onto all the high definition screens in the TV section of the store. The picture was up for only a short time, but one woman was so shocked that she called police.

Prude...

ALABAMA: Here's a story with a Facebook angle. An Alabama man was arrested after he allegedly put a status update on his Facebook page that read: "Has any 1 else eva thought bout strappin a bomb on n walk n a police department n blow da [expletive deleted] up?" Montigo Arrington was on probation police, went to his home and allegedly discovered he possessed kiddie porn and.

Pervy numbskull!

GEORGIA: How stupid can one get? A 26 year old man who bought a pistol at a Savannah gun show decided to load it as soon as he got out in the parking lot.

Unfortunately, he was so careless that he accidently shot himself in the leg.

...Wonder if the moron wanted his money back??

KENTUCKY: Here's a weird one. A naked burglar covered in chocolate sauce and peanut butter was arrested after workers found him in a supermarket. Police say Andrew Toothman, 22, was wearing only a pair of black boots when he was nabbed in the Food World IGA in the town of Neon. Detectives found peanut butter and chocolate sauce on the supermarket floor and the manager's office, and the word "sorry' spelled out in NyQuil. Toothman was charged with both burglary and indecent exposure.

What a way to get your freak on....

TENNESSEE: A man on trial for a robbery used his trial lunch break to commit another robbery. We learn that Mark Burgin allegedly robbed a jewelry store of $45,000 in goods, while he was on trial for robbing a truck driver at knife point. The second arrest did not affect his trial because the judge kept the jurors from hearing about it…at least, until after they found him guilty.

Some people just can't help themselves from thieven'…

TENNESSEE: A police officer in Memphis has been suspended from the force for accidently broadcasting himself having sex in his patrol car. All 35 officers in his precinct and any civilian with a scanner were able to listen in.

Oh baby, Oh baby, Oh baby, Oh baby…

TENNESSEE: It has been reported that a golfer in the state recently hit a hole in one – however the "hole" being the mouth of a wife of a passing motorcyclist. The poor duffer badly hooked a 14th hole tee shot onto a highway where it bounced and hit a woman motorcyclist riding with her husband. Several teeth were knocked out and she received hospital treatment.

No citation was issued, but we smell lawsuit…

FLORIDA: We read that a Lakeland man should be given credit for being efficient. Why? Aaron Weber, 38, was arrested for allegedly stealing a tow truck, which he then used to steal other vehicles!

What an efficient ninny!

FLORIDA: A drunken man showed up at a County jail to visit his girlfriend, then refused a deputy sheriff's instruction to depart at the end of his visit with her. The man said he would not leave and told the deputy that he would have to arrest him to get rid of him. That is just what the deputy did – arrest him. Now he is closer to his girlfriend.

Bad break but he'll get three free hots and a cot!

VIRGINIA: The headline to this story read: "This guy's 'brief' stint in jail will grow longer." A shoplifter in Eastville was sentenced to serve weekends in jail for his latest offense --- stealing underwear. He was told that he would have to supply his own clean undies in jail. So Alvin Rogers, 33, shoplifted two more pairs.

A mental midget – but one with clean underwear.

NORTH CAROLINA: A man who is deaf was stabbed by a galoot who saw him communicating in sign language and mistook his hand signals for gang signs. The victim, Terrance Daniels is expected to survive.

The headline read: "A Sign That This Thug was an Idiot."

LOUISIANA: A woman claimed to be a victim of stalking after receiving threatening text messages, but Trudy Miller found herself in handcuffs after Louisiana police found that she had sent the messages to herself. Miller allegedly tried to claim the threats had been made by an ex-boyfriend.

Nitwit...

ALABAMA: A man suspected of robbing two banks in Woodstock blamed God. The accused bank robber told police he pulled off the robberies after he prayed for guidance in solving his financial problems.

You idiot that was Satan answering your prayers, not God...

ALABAMA: This taxpayer invented his own money and sent it to the IRS. Income tax protester James Turner allegedly drew up $300 million of his own "bonds" and used them to pay his taxes. The IRS was not happy. They had him arrested. At the time of his arrest he declared himself the "President" of the "Republic for the United States of America."

Hail to the thief, Mr. President.....

GEORGIA: They say that justice might be too swift in Murray County. A judicial board is investigating a judge who allegedly pre-signed arrest warrants so police could just fill in the blanks, regardless of probable cause.

That's a no no Judge Dredd!

LOUISIANA: A woman erected a Christmas light display outside her home featuring a raised middle finger laid out in yellow lights. She took the "finger" down when threat of arrest by police was made. However, the ACLU sent a letter to police maintaining that she had a right to "flip" the holiday bird.

Yep, freedom of expression is protected by the First Amendment!

VIRGINIA: An assault suspect was placed the back seat of the police cruiser, where he stole a pair of the police officer's footwear out of the police car in which he was being held. Victor Alvarenga, 39, slipped into the officer's Nikes and left his own shoes in the police cruiser. He was later slapped with a petit larceny charge.

How petty can one get – stealing a cop's shoes!

VIRGINIA: A Chesapeake man was jailed shortly after purchasing a new SUV, because the salesman decided the price paid was too low – and reported him to the police for theft. The customer, who paid $5,600 less for the Chevy Traverse than the dealer's bosses thought was right, spent four hours in jail before police realized the charge was a bogus one. The customer is now suing the dealership for $2.2 million.

The worm turns!!

GEORGIA: So sad! A 21-year-old man was killed recently when he tried to dash across a busy Athens highway and got hit by a car.

The man had fled from a nearby restaurant when he did not pay his bill. The young man had been dining with three companions at the Waffle House and was the last to leave.

An idiot killed by the dine and dash crime....Sad...

GEORGIA: A 40-year-old woman filed a police report, stating that her resume, criminal history and a blouse had been stolen by a ghost. The woman told Barrow County officers that a specter or sprite must have been behind the caper, because the ghost of her mother often visits.

Boo!

GEORGIA: Atlanta area school official Angela Cornett was arrested in a Walmart parking lot for allegedly ramming her SUV into a 17 year old girl standing in a parking space, trying to save it for a friend. Cornett reportedly claimed the teenager threw herself on the vehicle and falsely claimed to be hit, but police are not buying her story.

We had to destroy the village to save the village...

GEORGIA: It has been reported that you can have GUNLUV and be a FEMFTAL in Georgia, but having a BIGBRA or GAYPWR are no-nos. The Georgia Department of Revenue is under fire for rejecting some vanity license plates but not others, leading to freedom-of-plate protests. GOD4EVR, GAYGAY, LOVWINE and BELLY have all gotten the OK, but UTERUS, GOTBEER AND GODROKS are among more than 10,000 rejections.

Who knew!

GEORGIA: A judge has appointed a cracker-jack local attorney to defend a pit bull that allegedly attacked a neighbor's 5 year old child. The dog's owner surrendered his pet to Effingham County after it was accused of injuring the child. Pro bono attorney Claude Kicklighter will defend the canine at what is called, in that county, a "doggy death penalty hearing."

An attorney must be able to communicate with their client. Does the dog speak English or does Kicklighter speak pit bull?

SOUTH CAROLINA: A man decided to demonstrate the best way to shoot one's self in the head and accidently killed himself, police report. James Gagum, 43, was watching a movie when he expressed skepticism about a suicide scene. "That's not how it's done," Gagum said as he put his own handgun to his head. Believing the weapon was unloaded, he squeezed the trigger twice and heard two clicks. The third squeeze, however, unleashed a fatal bullet and his demise.

Please kids, don't try this at home!!!!

SOUTH CAROLINA: A woman in the city of Anderson has been accused of working as a nurse for 27 years without a nursing license. Denise Lollis allegedly worked at the same Anderson hospital from 1985 to 2012 after submitting false certification documents. We learn further that she even worked as a college nursing instructor.

All we can say is she must have been one good nurse...

SOUTH CAROLINA: We learn that a few moments after Lamarcus Williamson was sentenced to 15 years in prison for assault, he displayed his displeasure with the sentence by punching out his lawyer in open court. Attorney Dan Hall ended up with a split lip and Mr. Williamson got six more months added to his sentence.

Can we assume the 15 year tip did not deter him from committing another assault?

NORTH CAROLINA: Debra Johnson of New Bern admitted to the police that she got so furious at a soda vending machine that took her money, but wouldn't dispense her a soda, that she set the machine on fire. "I'll represent myself, 'cause I'm guilty," the unrepentant 43 year old told a judge at her preliminary hearing. "I don't need a lawyer to lie for me."

... *At least she is one honest vandal!*

NORTH CAROLINA: A woman in Myrtle Beach speeding along at 70 mph in a 45 mph zone refused to pull over when confronted by police. Instead, she called 911 and offered to stop if police would promise her $300,000. She was finally stopped and arrested. There was no $300,000 pay out.

Nice try, but no cigar, lady…

FLORIDA: They say police had no trouble "catching up" with this fellow. He was a homeless man covered in ketchup sprawled out on a busy Key West street, screaming profanities at passing tourists. Police maintain that he resembled a "human hot dog." He was charged with disorderly conduct and resisting arrest. He will spend a bit of time in jail on the two misdemeanor charges.

We finally get it…"catching up."…Like Ketchup! Ha!

FLORIDA: We have just read a report that alleges that Florida is plagued by suicidal arsonist squirrels! The report maintains that the furry rodents have been causing massive destruction across the state as they scurry across power lines, get electrocuted and fall to the ground in a fireball, setting brush ablaze in drought conditions. Power companies report that squirrels catch fire more often than people realize, jumping from wire to wire and creating electrical arcs.

...Does the Department of Homeland Security know about this?

FLORIDA: This felon may have broken some kind of record. Marcus Wayne Hunt was released from the Hillsborough county jail recently. He strolled out of the jail walked a few blocks and within 16 minutes he punched a man in the face and stole his $190 bicycle. Hunt was soon arrested for robbery.

It's apparent that he wanted to be back in jail...

ALABAMA: We learn that officials have banned the sale of "Dirty Bastard" beer. Why? Because beer can be sold in grocery stores and they do not want children exposed to dirty words. The Alcoholic Beverage Control Agency could not explain why "Raging Bitch" beer and "Fat Bastard" wine are OK – except to say they were approved too long ago for anyone to remember the rationale.

"Dirty Bastard" Double standard....

KENTUCKY: A 20-year-old from the town of Jenkins was photographed by his girlfriend siphoning gasoline from a marked police car's fuel tank. They were so proud of said stunt the girlfriend posted the photos on Facebook. They insisted it was just a joke, but Police Chief Alan Bormes maintained that anyone who would steal from police would steal from "just about anyone." Charges are pending.

Cretins! Facebook... Helping the dumb be dumber...

GEORGIA: A 340 pound woman pepper sprayed and spit on employees at a Piggly Wiggly grocery store in Athens, after they tried to stop her from stealing bacon, cheese, chicken and beer. Lonneshia Appling, 26, also punched a store clerk in the face as she left the store dropping cans of Coors Light.

Sounds like she was preparing a "Movable Feast."

NORTH CAROLINA: An argument over groceries turned violent when one of the participants decided to arm herself. She armed herself with her prosthetic leg. The woman who, is confined to a wheelchair, took off her leg and beat a 29 year old man so badly that she broke his cellphone and glasses. It is reported that other people in the home eventually broke up the fight.

....Those must have been some kind of groceries!

KENTUCKY: This was not the time to commit a murder. A Louisville woman was arrested after she shot an acquaintance to death just a couple of houses down the street from where a large crowd of media and onlookers had gathered to watch police who were investigating a double homicide. Police at the crime scene heard the shots and wound up shooting the woman suspect as she resisted arrest.

Wow! How weird. Four killings all on one block

FLORIDA: An allegedly intoxicated woman was so angry when her boyfriend tried to break off their relationship that she bit his leg until he bled. The 41-year-old Walton Beach woman then pointed a paintball gun at him and said, "You're not going anywhere." Police were called and proceeded to charge her with assault and battery.

Seems she should have been charged with assault and bitery...

FLORIDA: Joseph Rainier, 53, was pulled over for speeding in New Port Richey. He quickly pulled out what looked like a gold colored police shield and told the police officer, "You're in trouble." "No, you're in trouble," said Cpl. Donald Velsor, who arrested Rainier for impersonating a police officer and resisting arrest.

Birdbrain...

FLORIDA: A Palm Coast man became so enraged when a basketball rolled onto his property that he fired off a gun when a 16 year old boy came to retrieve it. No one was hurt, but Theodore Van Beveren, 56, was charged with discharging a firearm while intoxicated. It is also alleged that he has been inducted into the "grumpy old men" Hall of Fame.

The old coot...

FLORIDA: It has been reported that residents of Jacksonville had better be careful if they need to go to court. Why? The area's new county courthouse has failed fire safety tests for the second year in a row. The problem is so bad officials are considering closing the place and reopening the old county courthouse.

Don't yell fire in the new courthouse...

FLORIDA: A woman was arrested on domestic violence charges for allegedly beating, choking and scratching her boyfriend after he said no when she asked him to marry her. Nikoleta Karoly, 24, had reportedly been hoping that getting married would get her a green card. She is quite upset that she might get deported.

With a temper like her's deportation is best!

NORTH CAROLINA: Rodney D. Valentine, 37, who had been locked up for 60 days at the Rockingham jail refused to leave once he was released, because deputies declined to give him a ride to a local motel. So, he was arrested for trespassing and has another stint in jail.

Rodney was used to those free three hots and a cot!

U.S. VIRGIN ISLANDS: Women and their purses! How about this. Police in the V.I. pulled over a pickup truck for a routine traffic stop and were surprised to hear a baby cry. However, there was no sign of a child in the pickup. The driver explained that she was taking her week old baby girl to a doctor and had the baby zipped her up in her purse.

...Sounds like she was an undercover baby. But Why?

NORTH CAROLINA: A man barricaded himself in a Belmont hotel room and made two demands: a pizza and Paris Hilton's hand in marriage. Frederick Denny, 61, said he had a gun and wouldn't come out of his Hampton Inn room until his demands were met. Of course, Police broke into the room, pepper sprayed Denny and arrested him. By the way, Denny was drunk. He also had no weapon.

What did Paris Hilton have say about all of this?

LOUISIANA: We learn that thieves broke into a warehouse in Monroe and fled with about 10,000 water meters that belonged to city of Monroe, worth approximately $75,000. Police theorize that the crooks wanted the meters because they contain salable brass.

Yep, a mighty brassy heist....

VIRGINIA: This one is about a man who was quickly arrested. Here's the report. A Virginia man who was fed up with waiting for the results of some medical tests showed up at the Chesapeake Regional Medical Center with a machete and a can of gasoline, insisting on answers about his tests.

Yes, the pinhead was quickly arrested...

GEORGIA: A nincompoop asked his pals at an Augusta bar to set his head on fire by dousing it with 100 proof liquor and holding a flame next to it. His head caught fire on the third try. He was hospitalized, and police didn't charge him, believing he had already "suffered enough.'

Truly a hot head!

TENNESSEE: We learn that a burglar broke into the family home of Landon Crabtree, 8, and stole two iPads. The youngster used an iPad tracking device to help deputies find the missing goods four miles away, allegedly at the home of John Docherty, 46. The Sheriff Deputies report they then found other items at Docherty's home, including guns, cameras, jewelry, guitars and electronics. The loot had been stolen from homes and hotels between Virginia and Florida.

Wow, a real professional burglar done in by a kid!

FLORIDA: Here we go again. A Florida woman tried to use nail polish to remove the man in her life. Idalmis De Armas, 40, of Tampa was arrested on aggravated battery charges after she allegedly dumped nail polish on her husband's arm and shorts and set them on fire with a cigarette lighter. She then scuffled with police. Her husband wound up with several burns, but nothing life threatening.

Whoooosh!

FLORIDA: Security guards at Walt Disney World in Orlando made a 15 year old girl change out of her Tinkerbell costume, telling her she looked too much like Disney employees who pose with visitors. Their explanation, she said, sounded like a "fairy tale." The 15 year old, April Spielman said the incident "ruined her dreams. I just wanted to be Tinkerbell."

The theme park was afraid that thy may have had to pay her!

FLORIDA: A police officer already facing trial for stealing drugs got himself in more trouble when he ripped off his ankle monitor while out on bail and visited a strip club. Brent Wooddell was located and taken into custody at the Cheetah strip club in Pompano Beach.

Brent, You can't "Cheat" the ankle monitor people.

FLORIDA: A man arrested for robbery had one heckuva defense to the crime. He maintained that a lack of sex drove him to crime. The 25 year old suspect said he robbed a 7-Eleven only after his fiancée refused to make love with him.

Lame, lame defense…The Twinkie defense was better that this…

FLORIDA: A privately employed lifeguard in Hallandale Beach was fired for saving a swimmers life. Tomas Lopez was sacked, because the rescue took place a few hundred yards past the border of Hallandale Beach that had been contracted out to an aquatic safety company. Six fellow lifeguards protested the firing of Lopez and the company promptly fired them also. The next day the company relented and offered Lopez his job back. He said no. He had moved on.

The boss was a real scrooge…

FLORIDA: A Port St. Lucie woman spotted her cheating husband at a Walgreens drug store with his side girlfriend, so she attacked him with a tub of ice cream she had just purchased. We hear that the cheating husband was bruised and hurt while his wife was arrested on an assault charge.

An assault with a dangerous weapon, this time with Rocky Road!

FLORIDA: A prankster in Crestview put on a sheriff's department uniform, went to a woman's house and solemnly announced that her husband had been killed in a traffic accident. He then departed. The woman's shock turned to relief when she telephoned and reached her alive and well husband at work.

Talk about a rude and imbecilic prank...

FLORIDA: How is this for irony? A Florida man was charged with illegally feeding an alligator – which bit off his hand when grabbing for a fish the man was dangling in front of the gator's mouth. Wallace Weatherholt, 61, lost his hand on June 12 and now has to go to court where he will probably be fined for feeding the gator his own hand.

Chomp. Gulp. Swallow...

FLORIDA: We learn that Disney World may have risked Santa's wrath after workers asked a man to leave the theme park, because he looked too much like Santa Claus. Disney executives were upset that children were mistaking portly and white bearded Thomas

Tolbert for Kris Kringle and mobbing him for autographs while ignoring the park's regular costumed characters.

Ho, Ho, Ho….

FLORIDA: A strip club patron maintains he spent a mere $600 at a jiggle joint, not the $50,000 that was run up on his credit card. Lokesh Simon James, 32, insists in a lawsuit that he spent $600 on dances, tips and drinks one March night at Bliss Cabaret in Clearwater and was shocked to see the five digit charge on his statement. "Do the math," his lawyer, David Sockol, said. "It's impossible to spend $50,000."

Anything is possible in a strip club!

FLORIDA: A man suspected of stealing merchandise from a Panama City store was brought down to the local police station for booking. While cooling his heels in an interview room the man unscrewed a clock from the wall and tried to hide it in his backpack. He was caught on tape.

The idiot didn't know those rooms are monitored by surveillance cameras.

FLORIDA: One wonders whether this fellow was trying to train his pet to be a drug sniffing dog. A West Palm Beach man was arrested for drug possession and animal cruelty after police rescued his dog that had been locked in his car without food or water along with a pound of marijuana and a pot pipe.

Surely, it was a hot dog!

FLORIDA: A hunter looking to shoot a wild hog instead shot his girlfriend in the leg. Steven Egan, of the town of Brandon, told police he did not notice his girlfriend had left the tent they had set up—and he heard a sound outside he thought was a hog. Police did not press charges and the girlfriend is recuperating in a local hospital.

Mistaking your girlfriend for a wild hog and shooting her does not endear you to her.

FLORIDA: Police in Tampa discovered a marijuana growing operation in a large planter directly across the street from police headquarters. Police say they had no idea how the "Mary Jane" came to be growing in the city owned planter. "There could be a thousand explanations," said a police spokesperson, "whether it's through pollination or somebody decided to actually and intentionally plant it there.

We hear that many people love "Mary Jane."

FLORIDA: A man visiting a woman inmate at a county jail had the bright idea of showing his private parts to her over a video feed. We do not learn whether this turned him on or whether he wanted to turn her on. We do know for sure that the guards were not turned on and arrested him on a "lewd and lascivious" rap.

Perv...

FLORIDA: An Orlando mother devised a creative and destructive new way to get her misbehaving daughter to leave her room and go to school. She set the girl's bedroom on fire! Adriene Latrice Ashley allegedly shoved burning paper under her daughter's bedroom door when the girl refused to come out. We learn that the paper set a chair on fire, but no one was hurt.

Pyromania Mama…

FLORIDA: A 17 year old teen gave up on a gun point robbery of a convenience store in Daytona when the store clerk persuaded the teen to get a job. She then persuaded him to fill out an application to work in that very store. He filled it out and left the store. Instead of getting a job he was put in jail thanks to the personal information he filled out in the application.

So stupid! This is why we call the state Flori-Duh!!

FLORIDA: We learn that a 32 year veteran police officer was fired from the Miami-Dade police force after she was observed hauling two mattresses on the roof of her police cruiser while still on duty. The department was so outraged at Officer Sandra Lyles that they fired her even though she was just days from retirement.

We believe the mattress may have been for her retirement pad…

FLORIDA: Two women produced knives and robbed patrons of a restaurant after they tried to get the patrons and staff to give them money for flashing their bare breasts. Sadly, no one took them up on the offer. "Basically, when they were turned down, they kind of got a little rowdy," a witness said.

The headline read: "No thanks for the mammaries."

FLORIDA: We learn that arrests have been made of Tysheka Pink, 29, and Katrina Summerset, 39, who are accused of stealing more than $34,000 in high end lingerie from Victoria's Secret boutiques in Boca Raton and Boynton Beach. Allegedly the duo walked into each of the stores and produced a large plastic Macy's bag and stuffed it with bras and panties before calmly walking out of the store, officials claim.

A Macy's bag in Boca...How tacky...

FLORIDA: A Sarasota man was kicked out of a jury pool for sending a "Facebook" friend request to a defendant. Jacob Jock was selected to help decide a personal injury lawsuit resulting from a traffic accident. While he waited to be selected from a pool of jurors Jock used his smart phone to see whether he knew any of the people involved. After spotting an attractive female defendant named Violetta Milerman on Facebook he sent her a friendship request. Milerman informed her lawyer the next day and Senior Circuit Judge Nancy Donnellan dismissed Jock for ignoring her instructions not to search the web for background on the case.

So dumb!!!

FLORIDA: A lead footed man allegedly showed up at the house of a Port St. Lucie police officer to argue a ticket the officer had given him earlier that day. The furious speeder told the officer's wife he just wanted to talk to the cop "man to man." Unfortunately, he soon wound up speaking to a whole bevy of police officers, at the jail to which they took him.

You argue your case in court – not at the police officer's house, fool!

FLORIDA: A 15 year old Holly Hill boy grabbed a tomato plant through an open kitchen window of a home. Homeowner Angela Cartwright couldn't figure out why, until the boy gloated, "I have one of your pot plants." "I chased him and yelled, you stupid little brat. It's a tomato plant," she said. The boy was later arrested when Cartwright sighted him on a school bus.

Little half-wit!

FLORIDA: After a woman was hit by a car and left bleeding in the street, 41 year old

April Cottman rushed to her side and asked how she was doing. The victim could only mumble. Cottman then allegedly punched the woman in the face and snatched her purse. Yes, she was later arrested.

Man, that's cold...

FLORIDA: We learn that a group of thieves who had just burglarized and stole $500 in jewelry from a house in Melbourne tried to hide the stolen stash in an order of Chinese food, after they were pulled over by police. Unfortunately for the thieves it did not work. The first place the police looked was inside the takeout food boxes.

Did white rice come with the jewelry?

FLORIDA: A man has been accused of attempting to kill his girlfriend's cat because the pet interrupted him while he was taking an online test and made him get a failing grade. The accused, Marvelle Rucker, who allegedly tried to smother the cat with a pillow, was also accused of poking the girlfriend in the face after she confronted him about the attack on her cat.

...Temper. Temper.

FLORIDA: A jail inmate, being treated at a DeLand hospital, allegedly escaped from custody of authorities. Unfortunately, he made his getaway wearing a patient gown, in shackles and while attached to a heart monitor. Accused forger Michael Burke slipped out of a bathroom, but did not get far as he shambled down the street in his gown and shackles. Police soon caught him and put him under arrest for escape.

How large was the heart monitor? Was the gown open in back? Inquiring minds would like to know...

FLORIDA: This one seems to be about "Judge Judy hate." Janet Knowles, 62, of Jupiter allegedly attacked her husband with a hammer recently. Police report that she was "upset because Judge Judy was on television." She was charged with aggravated battery and using a deadly weapon. The police report does not reveal why she hates Judge Judy.

There are so many haters out there….

FLORIDA: This crime story was recently reported: A masked bandit in Vero Beach stole purses from two women playing at a Vero Beach golf course. The first victim, Eunice Messick said after her purse was taken from her golf cart she went through the procedures of filing a police report, canceling her credit cards and changing the locks at her home. Then the thief targeted another woman. "She saw a raccoon grab her purse, take it from the golf cart and carry it into the bushes," said course manager Bob Komarinetz. He followed the raccoon into the bushes and found "stashed loot from both heists.

A masked bandit, indeed!

FLORIDA: Here's a story out of Jacksonville. An 85 year old man foiled a would be armed robber by hitting him in the head with a frying pan and then sticking him in the side with a pitchfork. As the would be robber fled, Korean War veteran Bobby Smith called police. An arrest was soon made.

Don't mess with vets!

FLORIDA: We learn that a suspicious package in Jensen Beach was not sent by terrorists. The broken box forced the evacuation of the town's post office after a clear liquid started leaking out onto the floor. It turned out to be moonshine.

If not sent by terrorists, by hillbillies maybe ?

FLORIDA: A woman's life was saved by her breast implants. The facts reveal that her fiancé's jealous ex-girlfriend stabbed her in the chest and the silicone acted as armor to protect her. "That was the best investment I ever made," boasted the victim about her implants. "It was just really lucky," her doctor added. "Three months ago she would have been dead."

Better than a bust in the mouth....

FLORIDA: A man has told tax agents that he was not subject to mortal man's law but "resided in the Kingdom of heaven." Nevertheless, Russel Gentile of Melbourne was charged with filing false tax returns.

...Only death and taxes.

FLORIDA: A man wanted for violating probation in St. Petersburg was caught hiding in an attic after his two year old son told officers where he was. The boy blurted out the attic hiding spot, while officers were questioning his mom who was claiming she did not know the husband's whereabouts.

"....Hey daddy is hiding upstairs in the attic!!" Kids and their big mouths!

FLORIDA: Sheriff's deputies arrested two suspected shoplifters at an Orlando Walmart after one of them used a baby's car seat to take a swing at one of the arresting deputies. Unfortunately, the baby was still strapped in the baby seat. Jodie Willis, 25, and Megan Kelley, 21, were both arrested and charged with robbery and child neglect. It was Kelley's baby who Willis allegedly used as a weapon.

She could also be charged with assault with a deadly weapon -- baby....

ALABAMA: A Heflin city worker found himself face to face with a topless woman who attacked him. No one knows why Anita Henderson Harris sneaked into a city storage facility or why she went after the worker, who was able to get away and call police after struggling with the naked to the waist woman. Harris now faces assault and other charges in connection with the attack.

Girl gone wild...

FLORIDA: A man was arrested for allegedly stealing $43 off the walls of a Destin pub that is decorated with $1 bills. The arrested suspect told police he was taking the bills as "souvenirs for friends back home in Michigan."

Tourists! Can't live with 'em, can't live without 'em in Florida.

FLORIDA: A woman in the town of Hudson dialed 911 for help. She told the dispatcher that she was lost in the woods and was looking for a place to "pee." Pasco County Sheriff's deputies followed up on the call and found 32 year old Marcia Usher. She wasn't lost in the woods. Nope, she was just drunk in her own front yard.

Yet , another drunken dummy...

FLORIDA: An Okaloosa County man was arrested for grand theft auto. He said he did not steal the car. He said he just happened to find the car keys in a nightclub and then found the matching vehicle. Sheriff's deputies found the car at a nearby strip club. The arrested suspect, Carlos Ortiz-Ortiz, 29, was also charged with possession of marijuana.

What a surprise...

FLORIDA: A homeowner in Live Oak called police because he discovered that a strange camper van was parked in his front yard. A basic trespassing call turned out to be the start of a "drug bust" when officers uncovered a meth lab in the camper. An arrest was made.

D'OH!

FLORIDA: A man in Tampa was recently arrested. Teacher William Chaney, 33, was arrested for allegedly head butting a student twice in class. Chaney who was charged with child abuse and battery was "horsing around" with a 13 year old student and head butted the boy twice, police say. The second hit came because the boy said the first blow did not hurt.

What the heck are they teaching students in Tampa?

FLORIDA: Here's another one from Tampa. Sheriff's deputies in Tampa are searching for a woman caught on surveillance video walking out of a hotel room with a television, a bedspread, picture frames, an iron, an ironing board, rugs, a trash can and curtains. The room inside the Sabal Suites in Tampa was closed for renovation. We learn that the items, in total, were worth $700.

Sounds like she was furnishing her own home...

CHAPTER FIVE

ZANY BUT ALL TRUE CRIMINAL LAW STORIES FROM ABROAD

BANGLADESH: How's this for punishment? Officials in Bangladesh have sentenced a man who allegedly "married" a 12-year-old girl to walk down his hometown's main street naked with a brick attached to his penis by a string while facing his neighbors' derision.

Boy, this punishment should certainly serve the purpose of general deterrence.

THAILAND: Here's one for the books. Thai police recently arrested an underwear loving man who was holding 20,000 pairs of stolen women's underwear. The 48 year old man kept half of them in the trunk of his car, so that he could have access to them even on the go. "He smelled them all the time, even while driving," said a Bangkok police spokesperson.

Sniff….Sniff…. Phew!

VIETNAM: A Vietnamese man learned the hard way he had better keep his temper in check. The man had become so enraged over a baby crying on a flight to Ho Chi Minh City that as soon as the plane landed and came to a stop, he pulled the escape chute and tried to slide out of the plane. Now he owes the airline $10,000.

Again, we caution temper, temper.

CHILE: A thief in Chile was arrested after chopping five tons of ice from a glacier. Police suspect it was going to be turned into designer ice cubes to be served in drinks at upscale cocktail lounges in Chile.

How does one haul away five tons of glacier ice undetected??

FRANCE: A gang of thieves dressed as knights armed with a sword and axe robbed a medieval festival. They walked away with about $24,000 after using the axe to strike a worker counting the day's receipts.

SACRE BLEU!

ENGLAND: A young man has been caught by security cameras making a meal out of a leather seat on a bus. Police say the footage shows him biting a chunk out of the seat causing $314 in damages which he will be expected to repay if he is ever caught.

A meal at McDonald's would have been cheaper!

CROATIA: While at a McDonald's in Croatia, a customer dropped dead at the counter and workers just kept on serving burgers. According to reports, the woman suffered an apparent heart attack and collapsed shortly after entering the restaurant. When the restaurant staff could not revive her, they allegedly propped her up, put a napkin over her face and went back to work.

The employees never thought about calling the police?

CANADA: A Canadian man nearly killed himself while trying to squash a mouse. The man, at a campground on an Ontario lake, was trying to bash the rodent with the butt of a rifle – which fired a live round that grazed the man's forehead. The man told the police he did not know the gun was loaded. Both mouse and man survived.

The mouse sure got the last laugh in this one...

BELARUS: Teddy bears in parachutes cost two high ranking officials their jobs. The nation's authoritarian president, Alexander Lukashenko, who has been dubbed "Europe's last dictator," sacked a couple of top defense officials after two Swedish ad agency employees piloted a light plane into Belarus airspace and dropped 879 teddy bears wearing slogans championing human rights.

Lukashenko has no sense of humor...

NEW ZEALAND: Prostitutes in Aukland have been advertising their talents by using traffic signs to do public pole dances. Some are "big, strong people," said local council member Dana Lee, and "they have broken more than 40 poles in the last year and a half. It has cost thousands of dollars to repair the poles."

Hey working girls need to advertise too!

HUNGARY: Boy, this one is ironic! The head of Hungary's anti-Semitic Jobbik political party had to resign after he learned that his own grandmother was Jewish and had survived the Holocaust. "I learned that I had parents of Jewish origins," said Csand Szegedi, whose party asserts that Hungary should be open only to "pure race Hungarians."

Yeah right…

AUSTRIA: Austrian police didn't need sniffer dogs for this arrest. The police stopped three overloaded trucks trying to cross into Hungary – and it soon became clear what they were carrying: nearly 10 tons of stolen garlic.

PHEW!

GERMANY: We have learned that the city council in Cologne has officially pardoned 38 "witches" burned at the stake in the late 1600's.

A little late don't you think?

JAPAN: A 38 year old Tokyo police officer, who reportedly admitted to friends that he wanted to be a high school girl, was fired recently for allegedly dressing up in a sailor girl outfit and exposing himself to a 16 year old teen. The report indicates that the officer had previously been arrested for exposing himself in public.

Surely a pervy weirdo...

AUSTRIA: A nature lover's club in Austria set up a hidden camera to monitor wildlife. They report the camera did its job. The camera caught a local politician having some wild sex in the woods. The politician was not identified and it was not clear whether the woman was his wife or his girlfriend. The politician is suing for invasion of privacy.

There is no reasonable expectation of privacy at night in the woods!!!

GERMANY: A German man, on his way home from Oman, was stopped at Munich customs carrying 49 live exotic lizards in his luggage. The man declared the lizards were not for the illegal wildlife trade, but he planned to cook them. To prove his claim he offered to bite off the head of one of the spiny lizards. Authorities declined his offer, fined him and sent the lizards to an animal shelter.

Better hope you are never invited to dinner at his house…

GERMANY: A new advance in criminal crime fighting: Ear prints! Yes, ear prints can be used just like fingerprints according to police in Germany. That is how they caught a burglar linked to 96 break-ins. He kept his ear to the doors to make sure that no one was at home before entering.

He was caught by the ear!

POLAND: A Polish man broke up with his girlfriend, who was also his dentist, but still went to see her when he had a toothache. Anna Mackowiak gave her patient, Marek Olszewski, a heavy dose of an anesthetic and pulled out every one of his teeth. "I tried to be professional," she said. "But when I saw him lying there, I just thought, "What a bastard!"

…And that's the whole tooth!

AUSTRALIA: A government worker was hit by a falling light fixture while carousing with a male friend in a hotel bed. A judge ruled she is entitled to worker's compensation, since she was on a business trip.

Sounds a lot like monkey business!

ENGLAND: Barry Monaghan was loading flowers into the back of his car in Hornchurch, 20 miles east of London, when a carjacker grabbed his keys and jumped into the driver's seat of his Ford. The former firefighter clung onto the open trunk as the carjacker hit 80 mph trying to shake him off. Then he pushed his way through the back seats and got the driver in a chokehold. The thief ran off. Police are searching for him.

That Barry be one bad dude!

ENGLAND: We learn that a British man owes his life to a kebab. After James Hobbs was stabbed in the neck, he stopped the spurting blood with his lunch pressed against the five inch wound. He lost six pints of blood, but paramedics said his quick thinking was key in saving his life.

YOOOUUCH!

AUSTRALIA: This one is about con artists and kooks. Serge Benhayon, who has no medical degree, says he massages women's breasts as a cancer prevention technique. He also maintains that he is the reincarnation of Leonardo da Vinci. Benhayon a resident of the town of Lismore, has a 22 year old daughter who talks to women's ovaries – for $73 an hour – a treatment that is partly covered under the Australian Medicare program.

They are faking crooks…

POLAND: The headline read: "The Rapper and the Crapper." A Polish rap artist commissioned a giant statue of dog poop and had it installed in a Wroclaw park. Lukasz Rostkowski hopes it will encourage his fans to clean up after their pets.

This really isn't a crime – but it should be!

ROMANIA: Police stopped and cited a completely naked woman riding as a passenger on the back of a motorcycle. They cited her only for not wearing a helmet. Police say she accepted the citation and then rode off into the sunset, fashionably dressed in only a helmet.

Don't you wonder what this is really about? Publicity, maybe?

ENGLAND: British police stormed a pub, called The Feathers' in the town of Laleham, after they saw a poster brazenly advertising live music "from 4 a.m." However, no arrests were made. The coppers learned that the name of the band was "4 a.m."

OOOOOOPPPPSS...

AUSTRALIA: Police down under have recently urged citizens to be on the lookout for anyone making huge quantities of coleslaw or potato salad. They issued the alert after thieves stole 93 pounds of mayonnaise from a warehouse in the town of Whyalia.

Right!

CANADA: What a sad story. A trip to his bathroom did not turn out well for Port Colborne, Ontario resident, Alistair

MacPherson, who died of natural causes as he was turning on the sink's water faucet. The water flowed for three weeks before his body was found. MacPherson's family has beseeched water officials to waive the $600 water bill, but they have refused.

GLUG GLUG GLUG….

ITALY: A prison in Italy shortened the 15 year sentence of a 56 year old Mafioso to a mere one year sentence after the prisoner complained that he was allergic to the vegetables served in the prison commissary.

Those Italian prisons are so darn accommodating…

ITALY: The mayor of an Italian village that ran out of cemetery space has made it illegal to die! "The ordinance brought happiness," said Falciano del Massico Mayor Gulio Cesare Fava, who is trying to negotiate with a neighboring town that has room for some extra bodies. The mayor went on to say,

"Unfortunately, two elderly citizens disobeyed the ordinance."

So, where are those two taking their dirt naps??

ITALY: This one is about a lady who was too well endowed. Police report that a 33 year old model was arrested by Italian authorities trying to smuggle more than five pounds of cocaine in fake breast and buttock implants. She had arrived at Rome's airport, and her plunging neckline caught the eye of security officers. This led to a search and subsequent arrest.

Too, too much T & A....

ITALY: A 99 year old Italian husband is jealous, real jealous. The man who lives in Naples hopes to live to be 100. He is the father of five children. He got so mad when he learned that his wife of 77 years had engaged in an affair he divorced her, even though the affair had ended 60 years ago, according to the hidden love letters that he recently found.

He would have been better off not knowing....

ENGLAND: A 20 year old man was arrested for allegedly cooking a live hamster during a wild party in York. The student faces a charge of "causing unnecessary suffering to a protected animal."

Hamsters are "protected animals" in England? Who knew? So silly. Why?

ENGLAND: It may not be unusual that a school yard fight be set up on Facebook – except when the fight organizers are mothers! The Brit mothers argued online over a forthcoming party, then agreed to meet outside their children's school to "throw down." The ladies did fight at 9 am after dropping off their children, but were soon arrested.

Silly grownups –school yard fights are for kids...

ENGLAND: A man who was thrown out of a pub in Hullo for lighting up a cigarette snapped. He came back to the pub to menace his fellow drinkers with a roaring chainsaw. Dean Dinnen, 24, sent many of the customers fleeing from the pub while others tried to hold him off with bar stools before someone managed to subdue him. Police maintain that the attempted chainsaw massacre was fueled by drugs.

Right!!!

ENGLAND: Here's a chilling story from last Christmas. A British teen wrote to Santa and threatened to kill him if she did not get a BlackBerry, money, a new dress and – Justin Beiber for Christmas. The 13 year old threatened to "hunt down" Santa's reindeer and "serve their meat to homeless people."

OMG, that's too cold...

ENGLAND: Recently, a British man was arrested for using his laptop, sipping coffee and writing down the answers to a radio quiz. Unfortunately, he was driving while doing all of this.

So much for multitasking…

UNITED KINGDOM: Officials in Cardiff, Wales, have found a new and bizarre tool to keep teenagers off street corners at night. They shine special lights on them which make their pimples glow.

Makes their pimples glow….How dastardly….

IRELAND: Officials at Christ Church Cathedral in Dublin report that a precious relic, the preserved heart of St. Laurence O'Toole, the city's patron saint has been stolen. Nuala Kavanagh, the cathedral's director of operations, said several nearby objects made of gold were untouched. "It's completely bizarre," she said. "They didn't touch anything else. They wanted the heart of St. Laurence O'Toole."

…And it looks like they got it.

CANADA: When things go wrong for some criminals they really go wrong. We learn a Canadian criminal was late for his meeting with police. As part of his bail conditions, the 24-year-old convict had to check in with Sudbury, Ontario police. He was running late and parked his car illegally in a handicap spot outside the station house. That certainly got the attention of the police. Upon checking out the convict's car they found not only was he illegally parked, but they also discovered his driver's license had been suspended, the car had bogus license plates on it and he was carrying two counterfeit bills on him.

OMG! He hit the trifecta of criminal wrongdoing all in one day.

SWEDEN: An armed robber who held up a woman in Halmstad at knifepoint was caught when he tried to escape from a crowd of pursuing vigilantes by running into a building. Unfortunately for the robber, the building turned out to be the town's police headquarters.

D'OH!

SWEDEN: After two infamous Swedish murderers met at a high security mental ward, their romance blossomed in online chat rooms. “Vampire Woman” Michelle Gustafsson, who killed a young father of four, and “Skara Cannibal” Isakin Jonsson, who killed his girlfriend and ate some of her body parts have announced their intent to marry.

We wonder how long this marriage might last?

AUSTRALIA: Police are looking for “The Bumcrack Bandit.” Authorities say the female felon held up a hotel bar and the only clue is a surveillance video of the woman making her getaway with her pants hung low which exposed her butt crack (or “bumcrack,”as they say in Australia). Police are now asking the public’s help in identifying the behind behind the theft.

Bumcrack?

SWEDEN: We learn that a Swedish train passenger was sentenced to prison for getting high and taking off his clothes. The unidentified man was travelling from Gothenburg to Orebro when he got high on pot, took off his clothes and walked through the train asking other passengers to have sex with him.

Did he ask both women and men to have sex with them?

GREECE: Greek police have reported that a childless former police officer invented 19 bogus children in order to claim benefits for all of them. He has been arrested. Officials contend that the 54 year old divorced man quit his $1,300 a month job in 2001 and had been living on the benefits.

Father Fraudster…

GREECE: A Greek priest was arrested after he was caught digging for treasure under the altar of his own church. Neighbors alerted police of the priest's activities after they heard him drilling at night at the Church of the Prophet Elijah in the town of Eyska. The Priest's treasure hunt has been one of many reported lately in Greece since the country has been hit with huge economic woes, because of its debt problems.

Maybe the holy man had staked a claim on everything under the altar!

EGYPT: "Brainy" smugglers? Egyptian customs officers confiscated 420 pounds of frozen cow brains that three Sudanese travelers were trying to sneak into the country. The brains, considered a tasty menu item in restaurants, could have netted the men $1,500, but were confiscated because authorities could not be certain that the brains had been properly preserved.

They could have used Igor's help…

SYRIA: We hear that one of the world's top paid soccer stars has been drawn into the Syrian government's propaganda war. Lionel

Messi, star for the team in Barcelona, Spain, has been accused by a TV station aligned with Syria's Assad regime of signaling smuggling routes to rebels in the way he passed the soccer ball on the field.

Yes, this is certainly something the Assad regime would believe...

INDONESIA: Authorities here discovered 1,495 pig nosed turtles in two pieces of baggage heading out of the country. The turtles, considered an endangered species, can grow as heavy as 44 pounds and are a favorite of smugglers. Authorities surmise that the turtles were being transported for resale.

You think!!

MEXICO: A would be bank robber rode up to a bank in Mexico City on a skateboard and announced a robbery. He may have made a strange getaway on his skateboard, but the teller set off a silent alarm and the robber waited while she counted out the money. Police then showed up and arrested the man.

Ninny – this is no way to use a skateboard!

GERMANY: Police in Germany were shocked when they caught the North Korean ambassador fishing illegally in a stream. When he was told to pull his pole out of the water he brazenly declared he had diplomatic immunity and kept his line in the water. After ambassador Ri Si Hong arrogantly waved authorities away, one police officer told reporters, "My colleagues are extremely frustrated."

Yeah, diplomatic immunity does that to people…

TAIWAN: What a way to go. After a video game player dropped dead of a heart attack at an internet café, nine hours passed before any of the other gamers noticed. Chen Rong-yu had been playing for 23 straight hours before he collapsed on his keyboard. No one even realized anything was wrong, until rigor mortis had set in.

So sad…So sad…So dead…

BRAZIL: A man held up a sex shop in Brasilia, walking out with a $4,000 gold plated vibrator. The clerk, noting the bandit forgot the charger, said, “I really don’t know what he”ll do with it. I’ll leave it to his imagination.”

Sounds like no Bbbbbbbbzzzzzzzzzzzz.....

GERMANY: A man in Berlin called police to complain that the woman he took home for a one night stand was demanding too much sex! We understand that he had to lock himself on his apartment balcony to avoid her loving advances. He called 911 and amused police officers showed up to save him from his predicament.

We always heard that it was the man who wanted more...

AUSTRIA: Police are on the lookout for two thieves for what is being called a “caffeine caper.” The thieves made off with 2 tons of coffee beans. The thieves had broken into a coffee roaster’s warehouse in Vienna and left with $72,000 worth of coffee beans.

That haul will keep them awake for a while...

SWEDEN: A Swede sent a number of Twitter messages to his local police station complaining that there were frequent speeding drivers on his street and that law enforcement should crack down on such dangerous law breakers. The next day police on patrol pulled him over in a speed trap and wrote him a $358 summons for speeding and dangerous driving.

Be careful what you tweet for, you might get it...

CANADA: A disorderly drunken man in Brockville, Ontario, who was thrown out of a bar by police, broke away from the officers, jumped into a car and ordered the driver to "get out of here." Unfortunately, it was an unmarked police car. We hear that his great escape ended quickly…and badly.

Our last drunken dummy!!!

ENGLAND: After a British man suddenly changed his Facebook status to "single," his girlfriend stole his car and crashed it at high speed through the glass doors of the bowling alley where he works. No one was hurt when jilted Claire Holley rammed the place. However, her boyfriend should "unfriend" her for his safety.

ZOOM, ZOOM, CRASH, BOOM……….

ENGLAND: Two police officers noticed a little dog, not breathing, on the back seat of a parked car. They broke in to save the little puppy which turned out to be a stuffed toy. "They must have felt like idiots," said Gordon Williams, the owner of the car.

They were idiots!

EGYPT: A husband in Cairo watching a pornographic film was startled when he recognized the woman in the steamy sex scenes – it was his wife! When he confronted his wife of 16 years and the mother of their four children, at first she denied it was her in the film. However, she relented and finally told the husband that she had never loved him and that the man in the film was an old boyfriend she had before she got married.

Instant marriage on the rocks, or poetic justice?

CANADA: We learn that an accused robber in Halifax, Nova Scotia, derived too much pleasure from his ill-gotten loot. The knife wielding thief demanded prescription pills from a pharmacist, police report. He swallowed most of the pills before fleeing the pharmacy. Police report further that they found him a short distance from the pharmacy – passed out "cold."

He who lives by the pills gets caught by the pills…

CANADA: We hear that a thief has found a new criminal specialty. The so called "Tailgate Bandit" has been annoying Calgary pickup truck owners, stealing dozens of tailgates from their vehicles. Tailgate theft is soaring, because an experienced bandit can pop one off in less than 30 seconds and sell it for $4,500.

…More lucrative than cattle rustling.

THE END

About the Author

Professor Birdsong received his J.D. from the Harvard Law School and his B.A. from Howard University. He teaches law in Orlando, Florida.

After graduation from law school he worked four years at the law firm of Baker Hostetler. He then entered into a varied and distinguished career in government service. He served as a diplomat with the U.S. State Department with various postings in Nigeria, Germany and the Bahamas.

Professor Birdsong later served as a federal prosecutor. After leaving government service, and before he began teaching, Professor Birdsong was in private law practice in Washington, D.C.

www.BirdsongsLaw.com
lbirdsong@barry.edu

Ordering Information

New books coming soon!

Dear Reader,

If you liked this book, I would greatly appreciate you writing me a review on Amazon or any other book site.

I look forward to sharing more funny stories with you in future books.

Thank you, I really appreciate your help.

Regards,

Professor Birdsong

Winghurst Publications
1969 S. Alafaya Trail / Suite 303
Orlando, FL 32828-8732
www.BirdsongsLaw.com
lbirdsong@barry.edu

Other books by Professor Birdsong:

- Professor Birdsong's 147 Dumbest Criminal Stories: Florida.
- 177 Dumbest Criminal Stories – International.
- Professor Birdsong's 157 Dumbest Criminal Stories.
- Professor Birdsong's Weird Criminal Law Stories.
- Professor Birdsong's "365" Weird Criminal Law Stories for Every Day of the Year.
- Professor Birdsong's Weird Criminal Law Stories, Volume 2: Stories From Around the States and Abroad.
- Professor Birdsong's Weird Criminal Law Stories, Volume 3: Stories from New York City and the East Coast.

- Professor Birdsong's Weird Criminal Law Stories - Volume 4: Stories from the Midwest.
- Professor Birdsong's Weird Criminal Law Stories, Volume 5: Stories from Way Out West.
- Professor Birdsong's Weird Criminal Law Stories - Volume 6: Women in Trouble.
- Professor Birdsong's Weird Criminal Law - Volume 6: Women in Trouble!
- Immigration: Obama must act now!
- Professor Birdsong's 77 Dumbest Criminal Stories.
- Professor Birdsong's Dumbest: Thugs, Thieves, and Rogues.
- Professor Birdsong's LAW SCHOOL GUIDE: Techniques for Choosing, and Applying to Law School

www.ingramcontent.com/pod-product-compliance
Lightning Source LLC
Chambersburg PA
CBHW021152020426
42331CB00003B/29
* 9 7 8 0 9 9 7 2 9 6 4 4 0 *